Karl Staib

Visit
WorkHappyNow.com/book

**Get the free
10 week eCourse to help you create a happier
and more successful you.**

Karl Staib
Work Happy Now

ISBN-13: 978-1477532492
ISBN-10: 1477532498

www.WorkHappyNow.com

A List of Passion Expanders

1. Work Resolutions

2. Superpowers

3. Relationships

Dedication

To my loving wife, Nikki Staib, who has put up with my crazy idea of wanting everyone to be happy at work.

Your Happiness Foundation

> *"I can tell you what I believe is the secret to a happy life,"* Justice Sandra Day O'Connor said. *"Work worth doing."* (1)

I am not happy in the typical sense. I don't skip around work, laughing and giggling all day long. Happiness to me is learning from each moment, whether it be dealing with a difficult project or running a workshop.

Work can be very hard. From a complicated task to dealing with other people, there are always moments that will frustrate you.

Work happiness all starts with your mindset. If you can find little joys in your work then you can create a positive mindset that leads to great work. You also have to believe that what you are doing makes a difference in people's lives. This connection will help you stay focused on the value of the work instead of letting yourself get caught up in what you don't like about your daily tasks.

Believe me you don't want to miss the happy plane because you are focused on the wrong things. You need to focus on your superpowers. Using your superpowers means that you are doing work that you are passionate about, staying focused and playing to your strengths.

Why this book will help you

Work happiness starts from the inside out. After talking to hundreds of people about work happiness, I've come to the realization that work happiness is 100% the individual's responsibility. If a person isn't happy, they need to make a change.

The choices that you make create your external world in which you live. What you put into your work determines the level of reward that you get out. I'm not just talking about money. I'm talking about seeing results that make you happy.

You can't expect people to give you great work. You have to show off your superpowers and encourage others to utilize them. Your career is your business. The better you leverage your superpowers. the more valuable you become. The more valuable you are to others, the more leverage you will have to create a great career.

Foundation

In order to build your happiness foundation, you need to be more understanding of your needs. When you can appreciate what you need in order to feel happy then you can make it happen.

Yes, there are steps to achieving happiness. You have to smile before you can laugh.

You need to find what makes you happy at work and try to do more of it. When you are emotionally connected with your actions, you will be working from a foundation that will support your confidence.

This is where the book starts. You need to dive into your thoughts and emotions if you want to discover how to make your career into an amazing journey. The more you engage these concepts, the more enjoyment you will extract from your career.

You have to know how you want to feel at work. Do you want to feel exhilarated, relaxed, challenged? You have to know what makes you happy most of the time. Yes, your emotions fluctuate and no job is perfect, but you have to understand what you really want out of your career.

How do you want to feel while you work? (e.g. excited, loved, respected, appreciated, etc.)

The Three Pillars of Success

Please take 60 seconds to think of a recent accomplishment. What did you do well? How did you do it? Who was with you? Think about all the stuff you did right that put you in that position. The more you can discover why this worked for you, the easier it will be for you to attract success into your life.

Please write it down:

Without even knowing it, you probably used the 3 steps to make it happen.

The 3 steps to loving your career

- Superpowers
- Relationships
- Results

These are the core concepts underlying the Work Happy Now approach. You use them every day to move forward in your life. If you are finding yourself unhappy in your daily working life, perhaps you have forgotten to use one or more of these concepts.

Superpowers

You need to know yourself so that you can optimize your work and life happiness. During an important meeting, I was offered a donut. Now donuts don't usually sit well with me, especially before a big meeting. The person offering it to me had this big smile on her face like "you are going to love these." She said they were from a local donut shop that makes the best donuts in the world.

The old me would have grabbed one, stuffed it down my throat and suffered through an upset stomach. The present day me understands that if I do this, I'll be doing more harm than good. The sugar rush would send my energy level sky high only to plummet shortly after and I wouldn't be able to communicate at the optimum level. Instead, I accepted the donut so I would not depress the important executive, but I never took a nibble. I just ripped it in half to give the effect of it being nibbled on. She was happy that I didn't reject her. I was happy that I didn't eat it. We had a great meeting.

When you reflect on what makes you truly feel good, while balancing other people's feelings into the mix. That's the difference between someone with self knowledge and someone who doesn't listen to their needs. Individuals who listen to their needs and act on them will be more in tune with their superpowers.

Relationships

You need to create relationships that will help you, by building relationships with people who share similar goals. If you want to be a famous artist then start connecting with other artists, art dealers, potential customers. If you want to learn how to invest your nest egg then begin contacting other investors. The internet is filled with people who want to help and connect.

You need to surround yourself with people who can teach you and you them. The best relationships are ones that help more than one person. It's these relationships that will also spur you to take action as well as help you figure out how to get the results you need.

Results

I love working hard, but only on the stuff that I love to do. You probably have the same problem. You love doing tasks that fit into in with your superpowers and passions because it doesn't feel like work. You might not feel that you have this option, but you do.

Working happy now comes down to aligning your needs with your co-workers and customers. If you are able find a perspective within yourself that allows you to extract joy out of a task, then you've fought and won the hardest internal struggle.

If you want to reach the goals that you have in life then you need to create results that bring value to yourself and the people with whom you work. If you think before each project, "How can I bring the most value to others as well as myself?" the results will come.

Let's begin...

*(1) Excerpt from Gretchen Rubin's interview at the Happiness Project -
http://www.happiness-project.com/happiness_project/2009/04/the-secret-to-happiness-
according-to-justice-oconnor.html*

My Work Happiness Manifesto

Work happiness is as important as any other part of my life. When I am happy at work, it makes the rest of my life easier to enjoy. I'm not just talking about a 9 – 5 job. I'm talking about every aspect of action. Cooking a meal takes work. Reading a book takes work. Commuting home takes work.

If you love to cook then it is probably a superpower. You have a passion for it. You can easily get into the cooking zone. You also love the reaction that you get from the people you cook for.

When I'm happy, my stress level is low, my results are fantastic and I feel good when I'm in action.

If you can't enjoy the feelings that occur while performing an action, it's your own fault. Yes, it may be hard to enjoy some things such as a commute in traffic, but what is the alternative - hating it? We all have tough parts of our lives, but it's up to us to find ways to relax, enjoy, and create results that make us happy.

It's why I decided to create a manifesto. It has helped me take my success and overall happiness to a new level. My manifesto serves as a guide for my life. Now, whether I'm mowing the lawn on a hot day or walking the dog on bone chilling day, I stop letting the loop of complaining bring me down.

Constant complaining can drag even the most positive person down. So, I just think about one item from my manifesto and see if I can't improve my perspective.

Here is my Work Happiness Manifesto:

1. Share stories (Good and bad – a little complaining can be good for bonding).
2. Know yourself.
3. Watch your emotions (even when you're feeling down, your emotions can still be intriguing).
4. When you are struggling, ask yourself, "How can I enjoy this situation?" (Notice how your creativity takes over. This technique can help you focus on any tiny sliver of a positive).
5. Design matters. (A quality office chair is worth the price tag.)
6. Be weird (We are all a little weird: embrace it and let it out).
7. Seek out your purpose (When you believe in what you do, it's easier to do great work).
8. It's your responsibility to be happy at work.
9. Give honest compliments like they are going out of style.
10. There is beauty in every single moment (We just have to be open to it).
11. Find the fun in the game (Work is a game, from corporate politics to arbitrary deadlines. Don't take it too seriously).
12. Eating healthy food makes it easier to be happy.
13. Creativity is vital at every job (Otherwise boredom sets in).
14. Relax while you are listening (If you are too tense, you'll miss half of the message).
15. Trust your gut (Most of the time it will be right).

16. Stay curious (Work is more enjoyable when you're discovering new solutions).
17. "Work is overrated." – Jim Maloney (I agree if it feels like work, but if it's fun then there is nothing more exhilarating).
18. Bring back sensuality to your work (It's not just about the brain; work is also about our senses).
19. Try something new every day.
20. Connect with people personally so they open up to you.

I would like you to try writing your own work happiness manifesto.

Try to think of at least 5 things that you would include in your manifesto:

1.

2.

3.

4.

5.

How could you use this idea to improve your career and overall happiness?

By creating your own manifesto, you will begin the process of making your work happiness a reality.

Work Resolutions

In order to make my manifesto really mean something, I created resolutions that resonated with me.

They are:

1. Volunteer Your Superpowers and Passion
2. Laugh Often
3. Share Stories
4. Be Weird - (AKA – Let Your True Self Shine)
5. Stop Controlling and Start Steering
6. Give Honest Compliments Freely
7. Enjoy Every Feeling
8. Release Feelings Throughout the Day
9. Explore Your Curiosity
10. Practice Daily Appreciation
11. Try to Make Other People Happy
12. Celebrate Results

I'll break them down so you understand what they mean and you can learn how to create a work resolution list that will encourage you to take your working life to a happier level.

Volunteer Your Superpowers

To hone in on a moving target such as your happiness, there usually needs to be three reference points in order for the measurement to be exact. You can add a fourth reference point, but the increase in precision is minimal at best.

Your best bet is to focus on your superpowers. This requires understanding your strengths, passions and what you can stay focused on for extended periods of time. This works because if you just volunteer your strengths you may do a great job, but hate every minute of the experience. If you just volunteer your passions the opposite might occur.

You need to find a way to fuse your strengths, passions, and focus together to create a career that will bring you so much happiness and success that you wake up with a big smile on your face every morning.

The hard part is figuring this all out.

I figured this out by studying myself in the same way that a scientist studies a problem. It was a lot of trial and error. I started by writing my superpowers next to my hobbies. Always use verbs because superpowers and passions are about the joy we experience while doing certain things, not the result of completing the task.

Superpowers	Hobbies
- Discovering - Problem solving - Telling stories - Making other people laugh - Listening - Coaching - Teaching - Writing	- Hiking - Practicing Yoga - Walking the dog around the neighborhood - Grilling - Meditating - Landscaping - Drawing - Painting - Dancing - Playing Video Games

Once you are able to get a better grasp of what you enjoy, it's important to figure out how you can apply this to your career. Many of you may love video games, but you can't make money from it. Figuring out the formula that makes you happy is never easy, especially since it probably changes on what seems like a daily basis.

We all have core needs. These needs never change. They are hardwired into our genetics.

I believe that you can bring happiness into your work by uncovering these hidden needs and finding a way to meet them through your talents.

Pick three superpowers and any hobbies that might fit and look to see how they might fit together. How can you use these skills at your current job?

For example, I love to teach, so I asked an old boss if I could teach financial literacy to local high school students in order to spread the awareness of my company. My boss agreed and it became a regular part of my job.

You need to do more of what you are good at and what you enjoy doing. That may mean doing a project on the side or even asking your boss if you can create a special project or work on an existing project that will utilize your talents and passion.

By volunteering your superpowers to friends, co-workers, and people in need you get a better understanding of yourself. This understanding will help you decide the future direction of your career.

It's important that you share your gifts with the world. Optimize your gifts by finding ways to bring them to people who are looking for these talents.

What are your greatest superpowers?

How can you use more of them at your job? (Think about what you do well and how you can apply these superpowers in the workplace. You may love to write, so every chance you get offer to contribute the website, newsletter, or business plan.)

Laugh Often

Laughter is the glue of relationships. We make each other laugh in order to bring happiness into each other's lives. There are few things that are better than delivering a joke that makes a whole room laugh.

Here is a joke that I enjoy:

Don't copy if you can't paste! (1)

A popular motivational speaker was entertaining his audience. He said, "The best years of my life were spent in the arms of a woman who wasn't my wife!"

The audience was in silence and shock. The speaker added, "And that woman was my mother." Laughter and applause.

A week later, a top IT manager trained by the motivational speaker tried to crack this very effective joke at home. He was a bit foggy after a drink.

He said loudly, "The greatest years of my life were spent in the arms of a woman who was not my wife." The wife went wild with shock and rage.

Standing there for 30 seconds trying to recall the second half of the joke, the manager finally blurted out ".... and I can't remember who she was!"

This joke isn't "bust your gut funny," and that's my point. Even if it's just slightly funny it still makes you feel something.

I'm not much of a joke teller. My preference to make other people laugh is to play off someone else's comment. That's why I would make a terrible stand-up comedian – it's too much of a one man show.

I am working on telling stories that make people laugh. It's an art that can bring joy to a lot of people. One of my favorite storytellers is Zig Zigler. One of the best stories he tells is about how his wife convinced him to buy a house that was out of their price range. The story is filled with anecdotes that crack up the audience.

The best part about Zig is his ability to teach and entertain – without these two skills it's hard to be a professional speaker. He makes you feel good about what you are learning. I feel like I could hang out with Zig, drink some iced tea, and just chat for hours.

When you laugh together with a co-worker, boss, or a customer you create a stronger bond. These relationships will help bring fun to your work and friendships that you can rely on for many years.

Notice what makes you laugh or smile. (You'll be surprised by the wide variety of topics that make you laugh and smile.)

How can you bring more fun and laughter to your work? (Make a plan to spread more laughter around. It could be a self depreciating story, a practical joke or something simple like bringing in a picture of your dog in a ladybug outfit. My wife actually did this to my poor dog.)

Can you make this a weekly habit? Why or why not?

If you are able to make this a habit, you'll improve your mood as well as the people that you work with. When you have a happy friend you become 15% happier. When you are making people laugh it's a win for you as well as the people in your working life.

(1) Tension Not -
http://www.tensionnot.com/jokes/office_jokes/dont_copy_if_you_cant_paste

Share Stories

A few years ago I was sitting at my desk and hating life; the sounds, smells, and sights all annoyed me. I was letting my job destroy me. I wanted to run to my car and take off and never come back. However, if I did this I would be admitting defeat. *My job couldn't destroy me; nothing can destroy my self worth.*

It all started with a few simple comments from my boss:

"Why couldn't you see this coming?"

"Don't bother, I'll do it. You'll just mess it up."

"We don't need you on this project."

These comments ate away at my confidence and happiness until I was a shell of my true self.

A few comments turned into a dozen, and then two dozen.

Regardless of the situation, one can learn from any pain and actually turn a negative into a positive. I found reserves within myself that gave me strength.

The definitive moment came when I was sitting in my car on a lunch break, ready to just walk away for good. I looked out my side window and noticed a hoard of napkins floating across the parking lot. The mother of three kids just stood and watched the napkins float away. She knew that running after them would be a waste of her efforts. The wind was too strong, so she just watched. I could see that she was upset that she was littering the world with napkins, but she didn't have the option of running after them while having to watch three little kids. The flying napkins triggered the beauty I had been ignoring. My life had beautiful moments if I took the time to see them. In those thirty minutes before I had to go back to work, I wrote three poems and released every ounce of my pain. The words poured out of me.

I shared these poems with friends, co-workers and anyone who would read them.

By creating this emotional release, I became stronger and realized that no one could take my superpowers away from me. I couldn't afford to let anyone crush me.

I opened myself to the possibilities that were right before me. I found a new job and never looked back.

I tell my clients to let their employees go if they want to move on. It doesn't do the company or the employee any good if they are ready to move on. That's why more companies should have career talks with their employees. When you can find out what their dreams and hopes are you have a deeper understanding of what motivates them.

If you aren't happy you have to understand why. Once you understand your "why" that's when you can construct a plan to make yourself happier.

What happiness have you been ignoring because you've too busy complaining?

Make a list of three people you can share these stories with:

Take the time to call or chat with these people about these ideas. Notice how it spurs them to find similar stories. You'll be helping them, as well as yourself, to remember and apply these stories to your career. It's these memories that will give you the tools to be happier and more productive.

Be Weird (AKA – Let Your True Self Shine)

Own your true self and people will accept you.

I don't mean that you should sit in the corner cackling like a crazy man while finishing your nineteenth cup of coffee. What I mean by "be weird" is to let your true self shine. You've seen kids before they are conditioned by society to fit in. They make crazy noises, say exactly what's on their mind, and believe in the wildest stories. Hugh Macleod of the Gaping Void (cartoonist/writer) -- hope he doesn't take this the wrong way -- is weird.

He makes it work.

I saw him speak at a South by Southwest conference panel in 2009, "From Blog to Book Deal: How-To." He threw around the "F" bomb, made off hand comments about creativity and drinking, and laughed at people's questions. Overall he was awesome. His quirky side came shining through.

Many of us don't have the confidence or credentials to let our true weird selves out. *Or so we think.* We are constrained by what we think other people want. Instead of telling a joke that will give us delight, we hold back because of the reaction other people might have.

Baaaaah!

I'm guilty of this too. I refrain from overloading people with a bunch of nonsense that only makes me laugh. The problem is that I hold back way too often. When I was a kid I used to say 90% of what was on my mind, and then as I hit my teens I pulled back to 30%. *Of course these are guesstimates.* As I get older, I increase my percentage. I feel more comfortable saying something without worrying about what other people think.

The older we get, the closer we need to get to that 99% threshold. We need to get closer to that time when we were kids and not worried about social repercussions. If people don't like our perspective then they are free to hang out with other people.

Being our true selves at work and at home will bring more happiness than almost anything in our lives. We are accepting our true selves and allowing other people to accept our true selves too.

This love for your true, beautifully weird self should be let freeeeeeeeeeeeeeee.

What part of your personality are you most afraid of? (e.g. small talk, joke telling, sharing feelings...)

Why are you afraid of this part of yourself?

What ritual can you develop to become more comfortable with this part of your personality? (If you are uncomfortable with small talk how can you put yourself in a position to use your superpowers in this area? For example I have a friend who is terrible at business meetings, but great at lunches, so she only does lunches. Remember you can't always be something that you are not, so sometimes you just need to stick with your strengths.)

Stop Controlling and Start Steering

A few years ago my happiness was all about control. Then I wised up. I began to notice when I had control over a situation and when I did not. By my best estimate, I had control over 50% of my life (100% of how I reacted to my life), but only .00000000000000001% over everything else. That's probably understating it. I can't control whether my co-workers are in a good mood or whether my dog runs after a squirrel on our walk, or...

There are times when I have tried to control my reaction to a difficult problem in my life. A few years ago I was right in the middle of a blog post that was three pages long, and I totally forgot to save it. My computer crashed. Since my computer only automatically saves every 15 minutes I lost half of my article.

I growled, stood up and paced the room to subdue these feelings. I couldn't. I tried to get back to rewriting the article, but my emotional stability was lost. I gave up and never returned to the article.

I thought that I could be a task master, a man built around self discipline, but this method only made me hold tighter and get upset at any small change. I needed to reframe my perspective. I was able to do this by thinking of my emotions not as something that needed to be controlled, but rather as something that could be steered in the right direction.

Steering instead of controlling has worked wonders for my happiness. A few weeks ago the exact same situation happened. I forgot to save my article and my computer froze. I lost half of my blog post. You would figure I would have adjusted my automatic save settings, but I didn't.

Instead of trying to control my emotions, I growled, paced, and took a bathroom break then started steering my emotions back to safe territory. I thought about what I wanted to write and I knew I had the concept still in my head so I tried to improve on what I had written just a few minutes before.

It worked!

My emotional steering allowed me to experience the feelings, but then I was able to focus my thoughts on the positives that could be extracted from the situation.

When you try to control how you react to a situation, you suppress instead of processing your feelings. You can't dictate your feelings. You need to allow yourself to experience your feelings, then steer them in the direction that will bring you back to a happy state.

What do you do to hold back your feelings?

How can you relax with your feelings so you are able to enjoy them and process them a little faster?

Give Honest Compliments Freely

Gratitude is the best happiness booster a person can use. When you give gratitude to someone else, you boost your own happiness as well as the person who receives it. Giving a compliment is a win-win.

The art of giving a good compliment is the fun part. People can only hear that they are awesome so many times before they tune you out. In order to give a good compliment, a person must be observant and willing to dispense praise without hesitation.

Praise the hard work, not just the outcome

The biggest difference between a good compliment and a weak compliment is how it's delivered. Even if it's honest, a person must praise the person's hard work, not just the talent. For example, if a co-worker does a detailed job on a report and hands it over to you, you need to thank them for their hard work. You want to make sure that they know you appreciate all the time they put into the final product.

Then find a way to praise the details within the work. People love when you notice the small things that other people miss. They see that you see the big picture.

Be honest

Every good compliment is honest. I've been given many false compliments and I can always see right through each one. I've also given false compliments and felt terrible as the words came out. I said what I thought the other person wanted to hear. I was too lazy to find a way to give an honest compliment.

Put detail in the compliment

The best compliments have detail within them. I received a compliment from a friend who told me that I always give thoughtful advice. He told me that he always looks forward to talking to me over the phone because he knows that he will feel good when the conversation ends. I could feel the honesty and appreciation in those two sentences.

Be Creative

A compliment should always be creative. One of my favorite compliments of all time was from my 12th grade English teacher. She told me that she would never forget me. I made such an impression on her that she would always remember me. I took this as a positive. I was a bit of an attention seeker, causing trouble here and there, but always to make the class more fun for the whole group.

Keep Notes

I'm not sure about your memory, but as I get older only so many things stick. If someone does something nice for me or does a great job, I try to write it down. This is vital for a boss/manager. If you are in charge of 7 employees plus your own work, it's a good idea to jot down the positive results that each employee has accomplished. When evaluations come back around, you'll have a reference point to review.

Give Freely

My parents never gave compliments freely when I was younger, and at times I notice that I fall into the same trap. I have been practicing giving compliments more freely, especially when someone goes out of their way to help me. I want the person to know that I appreciated the effort.

Practice

The more we give compliments, the more we will increase our compliment Karma. People realize that you care and they will show you the respect that you deserve as well as be more likely to compliment you when you deserve it.

It's amazing to see how much your work happiness will improve when you get into the habit of giving honest compliments freely. Because you are taking notice of other people's great work, you'll be more likely to take notice of the great work that you do and you'll create internal dialog that encourages amazing work.

What type of reminders could you create to remember to give more compliments? (I like to use my calendar that sends me an email. Because it goes to my inbox I think of a person and send an email, give the person a call, or write a hand written note.) It only takes five minutes, but makes a huge difference in my relationships.

Enjoy Every Feeling

Being passionate at work is all about feelings. If you feel excited about the work that you do and you allow each experience to help you grow, then happiness will come easily.

The easiest way to increase your happiness at work is to find a perspective that makes it possible. You've seen movies and TV shows that portray a tortured soul in a dead end job. Heck, you probably have a friend like this. They do the job for their family. They believe the sacrifice is worth the pain.

Maybe you are in that position right now.

I'm not saying that you have to be a martyr, but you do have to find a perspective that allows you to optimize your happiness at work. If you work at a job that allows you to be creative, then a grumpy boss might be worth the pain (A boss who bullies is never worth it).

At every job I've ever struggled with, I look back on the pain and I'm able to see that I failed to connect my own personal needs with the work that I performed. Even if I had to stuff marketing bags by the thousands, there was a way to find a connection.

I literally had to stuff thousands of marketing bags at a job that I had. At first, I dreaded the task and I could literally feel my shoulder muscles tense when I anticipated the work. I looked for reasons to hate the task. I replayed these reasons in my head over and over again. I was torturing myself because I thought I deserved it.

I needed to find a perspective that would help me enjoy the process without making myself depressed.

I turned the task into a meditation. I tried to focus on every sensation. How the plastic bags felt on my fingertips, the rhythm of my breath, the thoughts that entered and left. Everything was meant to be experienced, not hated.

I focused so hard on this skill that I created positive feelings every time I had to stuff marketing bags. I retrained myself to feel differently about this action by focusing on feeling every bit of the moment.

You can redirect the way you perceive a situation by focusing on the things that you can enjoy.

Next time you find yourself hating a certain situation, notice how you are feeling and what thoughts are causing these feelings.

Walk yourself through the process.

What is the situation that caused intense feelings?

What thoughts did you have immediately afterward? (e.g. You tell yourself how awful you are and why this is so or you try to ignore your thoughts)

What were your physical reactions? (e.g. clenching your fists or flashes of feeling hot)

How can you refocus these thoughts to bring more enjoyment out of a difficult situation?

Release Feelings throughout the Day

Feelings will occur as long as you are alive. Being happy at work is not about controlling how you feel, but using the feelings that arise. I used to believe that if I held on to a feeling long enough I would stop making the same mistakes. I was torturing myself into trying to be self disciplined. In reality I was bullying myself.

My feelings would fester and cause anger.

It wasn't until I learned to let go of the bad (and even the good) feelings and brought myself back to an emotional center that I improved my emotional intelligence. I practiced this by watching my thoughts carefully, and I stopped trying to control my thoughts so much when they would create various feelings.

I was like a cat playing with a mouse. Not there for the kill, but to just hone my skills. When a thought popped in and created a feeling I would notice it, process it, and then let it go by focusing back on the present moment. I was creating an emotionally balanced state. I stopped letting little and big things bother me.

During a bad economic time, I was worried that I might lose my job. My thoughts kept coming back to this fearful state. When a thought popped in I would try to enjoy the rush of adrenaline that would occur, smile at its lack of control over me, and then bring my focus back to my breath. This confidence was imaginary at first, but this practice actually helped me stay relaxed and extract as much joy from my job as I could. Again and again I applied this and I became more balanced throughout the years.

Now I feel like I can handle any difficult situation at work and release troubling feelings because I've put so much practice into staying emotionally balanced.

Most happiness gurus will tell you that the reason you can't be happy is because you worry about the past or future instead of enjoying the now (Reflecting is not the same thing as worrying. Reflecting is a learning process without attachment to outcomes or failures and worrying is the vicious circle of negative thinking). I took this simple knowledge and applied it to every dreaded task. Every time my thoughts drifted to other topics I gently brought myself back and tried to enjoy my movements, my breath, and the calm within the situation.

I literally trained myself to enjoy every feeling instead of worrying about what my life lacked. I didn't fully realize what I was doing, but I was teaching myself to find joy in every moment.

What feelings do you hold on to? (e.g. fear, anger, sadness, and even joy.)

When do these situations most often happen? (e.g. meetings, arguments with co-workers, difficult projects.)

What ritual can you create to let them go and bring yourself back to a balanced state? (Create a certain time throughout each day to bring yourself back to center and a plan on what you will do when you feel you are holding on to certain feelings.)

Explore Your Curiosity

I forget where I heard the phrase, "Only boring people get bored," but I love it. When we stop seeing the little things in life as interesting, we lose much of our happiness. Why do we forget that the simple joy in making a co-worker laugh creates a bonding experience that builds trust? We forget this because we get too caught up in our own worries.

The best time to explore curiosity is when we are worried. It takes our mind off our own problems and helps us focus on the people and projects in our lives. We think that our curiosity should be used for work problems like sales, accounting and marketing, but they can also help with physical and mental pain too.

Curiosity Comes from Feelings

It's why I started this workbook. I wanted to explore my feelings in order to help others find happiness at work and within themselves.

Curiosity is a brilliant solution to boredom and a great way to create more fun. You can bring more curiosity into your working life by connective ideas with possible solutions then trying to figure out how to bridge the gap.

For example, I noticed that my neck would get tight after a stressful meeting. I tried stretching throughout the morning and afternoon, but I noticed that my neck would still be tight by the end of the day. I could have just let it slide and hope it would eventually go away.

Or...I could get a little creative and try various remedies. During lunch, I drove off and pulled my car into a parking lot of a hardware store. I leaned my seat back and let my mind relax with the tightness in my neck. I began to think about the other people in my office and how they deal with their issues of stiffness, so I decided to talk to them for possible solutions.

I asked other people if they had the same problem and what they did to solve it. I learned various stress relievers and solutions. I began to check them out one by one.

The most important part to curiosity is not to have any expectations. If I expected each solution to solve my problem I would only have gotten angry and given up.

Ideas – test, adjust, and repeat

I tried music, various chairs, self massage and nothing worked. I was at the library and typed in neck pain and found a Yoga book about the alignment and positioning of the body.

I figured out that I was holding my elbows too far away from my body and it was putting strain on my neck. I practiced mixing up my elbow positioning and it worked. The book also suggested taking breaks more often and moving around. Within a few weeks, my symptoms subsided.

My stress was overwhelming me and I didn't know how to deal with it. If I would have kept ignoring this pain, I would never have explored my options. I have to thank my curiosity for pushing me toward a solution.

You probably have some physical or emotional pain. It's your responsibility to stay curious and have fun finding a solution. Believe me, not everything can be fixed, but the right perspective can sure ease the pain.

What gives you physical or emotional pain at work?

What solutions have you tried? Why didn't they work?

What solutions worked? Why did they work?

How can you get creative and unleash your curiosity until you find a perspective or solution that eases your pain? (Set some time aside to relax with your pain and let yourself explore various solutions.)

Practice Daily Appreciation

The technique that improved my happiness the quickest was practicing daily appreciation. I got into a bad habit of listing all the things that I hated about my day. I noticed that the negativity killed my energy. When I arrived home, all I wanted to do was numb myself with TV and alcohol.

I was in a vicious cycle of self-inflicted torture.

There are days when my negativity habits creep back in, and that's when my appreciation habit is my best ally.

During my commute home I try to list at least three things for which I am grateful.

Yesterday's list looked like this:
- Dark chocolate.
- My wife's willingness to help edit my articles.
- The painting of the Mona Lisa.
- Purple flowers of any kind.
- The advancement of tennis rackets.
- My dog's ability to jump and snatch a tennis ball out of mid air.

Some days I need to list 30 or 40 things, but by the time I'm done I'm always in a better mood. I never expect to feel wonderful after I'm done, but as long as I bring my mood up to a level state, then that's fine with me.

It's a foolish person who doesn't appreciate various states of mood.

Your focus determines your happiness. When you focus on the problems and you complain until you wear yourself out, then you create these upsetting feelings. If you focus on the good things in your life, you have a chance to encourage happiness.

What time of day would be the best time to list things you appreciate?

How can you make this so enticing that you make this a daily habit?

Start right now. List 3 things you are grateful for:

1.

2.

3.

Try to Make Other People Happy

Surrounding yourself with happy people will make you happy. I recently read an article in TIME magazine about the importance of having happy friends. The closer you are to a happy person, the more your percentage of happiness goes up.

There is a dilemma in this scenario – we can't always be around happy people. Our co-workers have bad days that can bring us down.

That's why we need to increase our happiness by encouraging other people to be happy. Why rely on other people when we can create the magic for ourselves? The best part is, even if the person who you are trying to encourage doesn't become any happier, you will.

It's the Karma of happiness. By putting your happiness efforts out into the world, you will be releasing endorphins into your blood stream. Endorphins are *the happy chemical that makes us feel good*. That's why it is better to give than receive. Not because you should, but because chemically we get more of a boost from making someone else happy than if someone makes us happy.

There are thousands ways to help others be happier:
- Giving compliments
- Offering small gifts (not too expensive, or else tension may form)
- Sharing a story
- Telling a good joke
- Building teamwork
- Suggest Stress Relief Techniques (offer to help another person with a tough project)
- Listening to their problems
- Offering a good website to help with their problems

The list can go on and on. Your happiness can expand if you help someone else become happy at work. I can cite about a dozen articles about the psychology of this process, but most of them are pretty dry and boring.

It's better to demonstrate by using an example that I know you've all experienced.

Laughter. Yes, the endorphin-releasing experience that we all love so much. When you make someone laugh, how does it make you feel? It makes you feel happy. It's a basic part of being human.

Making someone else laugh is the same as helping someone at work: when you do it, you increase your own happiness. You stop worrying about yourself and instead you focus on making someone else happy. The best part is that you improve your own happiness at the same time.

I finally found one quote that resonated with me:

> "When I'm feeling a bit down and I stop myself and say, 'Let's forget about me for a moment and do something nice for others,' the negative feelings subside, and a sense of bliss flows in to replace them. It's quite simple in practice. The challenge is remembering to do it."
> - Steve Pavlina's article **Afternoon of Life**

This trait is the basis of all good friendships.

What can you do right now to help someone (co-worker/customer) become happier? (e.g., write a "thank you" email, buy a small gift for a client, tell a story that will make someone laugh)

How do you think this will affect your mood?

Celebrate Results

I have always celebrated birthdays, holidays, and big wins, but I never took the time to celebrate my small victories. It's the nature of modern society. I never made time to rejoice in a good email or a great conversation with a friend.

Until recently...

It may sound weird to celebrate a great conversation, but it brings me a lot of happiness.

I try to remember to bask in the feeling of exploration that resulted from my small victory. For example, I was talking to my friend Brian about various work happiness concepts. He said that he often tried to hold on to failed projects. He hated giving up on them.

The light bulb within my own head shone bright.

I realized that I, too, hold on to feelings and projects. I often try so hard to push myself to victory that I stop having fun with the process. Having fun is vital to work happiness.

In the past, I tried to force myself to succeed when the foundation for success wasn't there.

I had worked on this internal issue for months without seeing great results. After having this one conversation with Brian, I fast-forwarded my emotional intelligence by a few weeks or maybe a few months.

Instead of just moving on, I jotted down a short list of thoughts.

As I listed each item I felt my happiness expand.

Here is the original list:

- I push or pull my emotions as I work on projects instead of enjoying the process.
- Brian triggered new cells to generate growth.
- I now know that I need to relax with my breath as I work. This will allow me to open my awareness to my thought process as I work.

Celebrating personal wins spurs me to do better work.

If you notice a twinge of excitement after completing a task, don't let this feeling just drift way. Jot down why you feel the way you do or at least take a moment to enjoy these feelings. I have a large plastic box full of little scraps of paper that I wrote poetry and business ideas on, and every once in a while I will filter through them. This, too, feels like a mini celebration. Seeing how I've advanced these past few years gives me more motivation to become an even better writer.

What small accomplishment have you brushed aside? Why?

How can you remember to celebrate the small things too? (Place on your calendar, set a timer for the end of the day, tell a friend about your accomplishments)

What are three small accomplishments that have resulted from your work? (e.g. a new contact, a great email, hard work on a difficult project)

How can you celebrate each of these small accomplishments? (Buy yourself a rewarding lunch, do a little dance, sit back in your chair and take a moment to soak in your accomplishment)

Your Work Happy Now Resolutions

You can also create a set of resolutions that don't require any external validation. That means that setting a goal of making $1,000,000 in the next ten years is out. You can set this as a goal, but I believe that resolutions should be attainable right now.

I know that we need goals too, but I believe that a solid foundation of resolutions will bring money, happiness, success, or whatever we desire into our lives.

So get started today. Don't overwhelm yourself; start with one resolution and practice that for a month. Then add another one. After a year you will have guidelines that will help you develop the life you need.

One of my resolutions that helped me become happier and more motivated was *be more helpful*. I was getting caught in the trap of what I didn't have compared to my co-workers instead of actually being helpful to others. This resolution helped me create deeper connections with my co-workers because I was actually helping people instead of just complaining about what I didn't have.

What would be your top 5 resolutions (not goals) for yourself while working? (Goals are finite; resolutions are guides to keep you focused on what will bring happiness into your life.)

1.
2.
3.
4.
5.

What is one specific problem you are having at work?

How could you apply one of these resolutions to help you with your problem?

Superpowers (AKA Your Medicine)

In order to build the relationships and get the results that make you feel great, you need to understand what you are currently doing right and wrong. It's so easy to say, but one of the hardest parts of working happy is actually practicing your superpowers on a consistent basis. I also describe this to my audiences as "you medicine" that you offer the world.

Superpowers are skills that:
1. You are passionate about.
2. Come easy to you.
3. Are strengths that can help you leverage your happiness.

You need to have all three to consider a skill a superpower.

To understand your superpowers, you need to break down your good, bad and neutral habits. Once you know what creates success and happiness, you can do more of it.

I emailed Seth Godin, the bestselling author of *Purple Cow*, *Tribes*, and *The Dip*. These are all books that I highly recommend if you want to separate yourself from the crowd (in your career or running your own company). I wasn't expecting a response back, but my question must have intrigued him.

My question: I'm working on a book, "Work Happy Now." I was hoping I could get you to answer, "Why is reflection so important to success?"

Seth's response: I'm not so sure it is.

My reply: I believe that without reflection you wouldn't know what your strengths and weaknesses are and how to maximize one and minimize the other. I believe success is about knowing ourselves and finding the best way to deliver this knowledge to people who need it (i.e. your blog and books). Without reflection, you wouldn't have changed the way the world looks at marketing/business.

Seth's reply: I agree. I think, though, that it's often an excuse not to move forward. Test and measure and repeat.

In the past I have often made the mistake of trying to over think a situation instead of diving in and failing, then fixing my mistake. But much of my hesitation was due to my lack of knowledge. I just wasn't ready, so I kept delaying action.

> *"Realize that HOW you look at things is every bit as important as doing those things."*
> - Chris Brogan, author of Trust Agents

That's why reflection is so vital to accomplishing great results. You need to keep adjusting your energy until you feel ready to do a great job.

If someone offered you $100,000 to hit a target at 25 yards with a bow and only one arrow, you would probably miss your target if you had never used a bow and arrow before. If you could invest $25,000 to have the world's best archery coach teach you the skills that you needed to win the money, would you do it? Before you answer, let's say that if you don't hit the target then you don't only lose $100, but if you do hit it then you would have to pay the person $25,000. You would profit $75,000. It's an easy answer. Most people would probably do it because you would increase your chances at winning.

You need to invest in yourself. You are leaving happiness and money on the table by not taking the time to learn or improve certain skills. You must reflect on the results that you are trying to achieve as well as the results you have achieved and adjust accordingly.

In my past situation that I described earlier, I wasn't able to take action because I didn't have the right mindset. I needed to find the inner knowledge that would help me shed my fears and try to succeed with the superpowers I had.

You need to take the time to adjust your actions by reflecting on the results of every choice that you make. Knowing yourself is the key to reaching your desired level of happiness and success.

Knowing Yourself

I read an interview with Chris Guillebeau, the author of *The Art of Non-Conformity*, which helped me understand the importance of knowing myself - superpowers, weaknesses, and everything in between.

Here is an excerpt:

Gretchen Rubin of *The Happiness Project* asked: Have you always felt about the same level of happiness, or have you been through a period when you felt exceptionally happy or unhappy – if so, why? If you were unhappy, how did you become happier?

Chris replied: I became happier by a) carefully examining a number of areas of my life that were not creating happiness for me, and b) taking a series of small-to-big actions to change that. Over time it worked very well. I feel like I'm in the 92nd percentile of happiness these days. I think I'd like to go to about the 98th, so I'm working on that.

In this section of the book, you will gain a better understanding of who you are and how to make yourself happier at work.

Oceans of Emotions

In order to be able to use your superpowers and focus properly, we have to understand the basics of how our thoughts and emotions interact with each other.

It's like being on a tiny boat on the surface of the ocean. When life is good, we lay out on the deck basking in the sun. When life is rough, we get bruised by the storm. If only we could turn our boat into a submarine, dive under the ocean and just chill until the storm is over.

That's exactly what you can do.

There is so much beauty and wonder underneath your emotions. Think about the last time you were in a bad mood and try to recall how one little thing helped you turn the corner to feeling good again. Maybe it was a smile by someone you had a crush on, or a good sandwich, or a quote from a website that made you appreciate your life again. This little external switch allowed you to turn yourself around to feeling good again.

You can do the same thing internally. When you are at your desk and life feels rough, you can go within yourself and find that calm feeling by reflecting on the good that is in your life. I prefer to anchor myself to my breath because it's always there. So when I'm upset, I breathe in and silently say to myself, "I am breathing in calm." When I breathe out, I silently say to myself, "I am breathing out calm." This sounds simple, but that's exactly why it works. It connects your thoughts and emotions back to your tranquil core.

All I'm doing is going underneath my ocean of emotions to a more basic place of joy. After a little while, I will send my little periscope up to the surface to look around and decide when it's safe to re-emerge.

This is why counting to ten helps people with anger management issues. It allows them to stop and reflect on what's important, instead of act on the anger.

It's important to work with your thoughts and emotions so they become your ally instead of that storm that pushes you around. You can easily do this by being aware of the moments when you have an emotional spike, then just allow yourself to feel your emotions rather than trying to change them or make them go away.

This exercise will help you bring more awareness to your thoughts. When you can dance with your thoughts and emotions, you can feel calm even in the lowest emotional dips. You are working with what you have instead of rebelling against yourself.

Next time you are stressed, afraid, angry, or even happy, try this technique:

When you breathe in, say to yourself, "I am breathing in calm." When you breathe out, say to yourself, "I am breathing out calm." This will relax you, but there is one more step. Notice your feelings before and after. Take mental notes on your progress. There will be a shift in your mood. It will be slow, but it will also be amazing.

After a few weeks of practicing this technique, watch what begins to happen. You'll be able to connect to your inner joy so much easier and faster. You'll dive within yourself to connect to that place within you that's calm.

What trigger can you use to reconnect with your emotional submarine that takes you to that calm center? (Do you clench your fist when you are super angry, do you shut down and want to be alone, do you get hyper and try to do too much?)

What emotional calming technique would work best for your personality? (e.g. journaling, deep breathing, puzzles, Yoga, meditation)

Personal Development at Work

Being happy at work means growing as an individual. The funny thing is that most of us don't equate personal development with our jobs. We see them as separate entities that don't belong together. I believe this couldn't be further from the truth.

The reason why personal development and happiness at work are forever linked is simple. The better we are at cultivating relationships and being productive, the more we enjoy our jobs.

Artists at Heart

We are all artists at heart. I watched a George Carlin interview. He talked about the importance of enjoying the various parts of his work. He couldn't just enjoy writing because his job also required performing and promoting (marketing). Everything was interwoven. He stopped thrashing against the promoting because it gave him a chance to do the writing. This awareness didn't come quickly.

George Carlin became successful when he began to understand who he was. In the early to middle half of his career he thought that he should be an actor because everyone else was doing it. He hated it. Success came easier when he stopped trying to be something he wasn't and figured out what really made him happy.

> "Happiness is a continuation of happenings which are not resisted."
> - Deepak Chopra

By not forcing yourself to do work that you don't want to do (being a big bully) and allowing your desires to pull you like a giant work-happiness magnet to do great work, the pain (stress and worry) will be significantly reduced and success will happen.

Your Career

When you take the time to develop your emotional intelligence and personal skills, you'll reap the rewards at work. The better you understand your needs, the easier it is to fulfill them. Next time you are caught up in office politics, denied a raise, or refused some much needed appreciation. Try to think of the situation as a chance to develop patience. Notice how it makes you feel and try to end the negative thought cycle and give appreciation to where you are at. You'll probably notice that by taking the time to improve your emotional intelligence, you will be able to enjoy your job even more.

What can you do to improve and develop yourself at work? (e.g. build better relationships, public speaking, writing skills)

How can you apply these ideas so you continue to develop your superpowers at work? (e.g. Offer to do tasks that push you outside your comfort zone.)

Developing yourself means implementing ideas from this book, but it also means learning from other people. Try reading something that gives you a new perspective on your life for at least fifteen minutes a day.

Four of my favorite personal development blogs are:

- StevePavlina.com (Forces a person to rethink his/her beliefs.)
- FluentSelf.com (Enjoy the beauty that is you.)
- Communicatrix.com (Struggle is a part of life.)
- ZenHabits.net (A simple life is an easier life.)

Being Happy at Work is not Due to the Absence of Suffering

The idea that a person who does what they love is happy all the time is a myth. Yes, they probably have an easier time being happy, but we don't usually see the complete picture.

You may hear stories from friends who love what they do and they probably make you feel a little jealous, but you don't see them during those periods when it's 10pm and they are stressing because a big project isn't coming together the way they hoped it would. If you had a chance to ask them right in that moment whether they are happy, most of them would say no.

The difference is how they use that suffering to make themselves smarter and happier. These painful experiences help us grow.

There is no way to fix your emotional state to feel happy all the time. Even the happiest people struggle at their jobs. As long as you understand that you will fluctuate between happiness and suffering, you can then work with your thoughts and emotions.

It all comes down to choice. You need to choose to use suffering to help you become happier instead of trying to avoid suffering altogether.

Next time you feel you are in a state of struggle, notice your reactions. What do your thoughts gravitate towards?

When I'm struggling, I try to stay with my feelings and notice where they are coming from, but sometimes I need a break by going for a walk in nature, practicing Yoga or doing something that helps me relax. I try to notice the beauty in the trees, flowers, and even my body in order to help improve my perspective. I also do this by thinking of the wonderful people in my life. Sometimes I need to focus on the positives in my life so that I can get a better understanding of why I'm struggling.

This practice helps me understand that my needs aren't being met. For example, there was a period of time when I worked for a boss who never complimented me. I needed to know the value of the work that I was producing. He only complained when I screwed up. So I realized that I needed to go to a co-worker to help me meet my needs. This co-worker gave me an honest assessment of my work. I found more confidence by finding a way to meet my own needs. I also found the confidence to quit the job and find a better place to work.

When was the last time you suffered at work?

What need wasn't being met?

How could you have found a way to meet your own needs?

Remember that if you don't suffer a little bit at work, you probably aren't growing either. So take time to learn from your suffering. You'll notice that you will be adding to your arsenal of emotional tools to help you release your suffering so you can feel good again.

Enjoy Your Mistakes

I've attended meetings where I've embarrassed myself. There was one meeting in particular that sticks with me to this day. I was fresh out of college and working at my first full-time job. My attention wasn't on topic when we were talking about marketing a new valve. I tried to insert an idea into the conversation and suggested we advertise on a certain site. Everyone glared at me as if I had just thrown up all over the conference table. My boss told me that I had better pay attention because that was just mentioned. I looked down at my notes and internally yelled at myself for being stupid.

My theory at the time was – the angrier I was at myself the less likely it was that I would make that same mistake. This technique wrecked my confidence. It took me over a month to recover from that incident. I couldn't shake off the dread of opening my mouth in a meeting. I was terrified to make another mistake.

Kindness – The Greatest Tool for Mistakes

Since that first job, I've learned to value being kind to myself when I make a mistake or have a lapse in judgment. I am now able to forgive my mistakes, which allows me to deal with the present moment. It's a simple tool to add to your life but one of the most difficult to implement. The best way to encourage self kindness is to use your mistakes as an opportunity to improve. When you have enough awareness to acknowledge your mistake, you've accomplished the hardest part. All you have to do is find a few things that could make your mistake helpful.

If you recognize that you have a short attention span during meetings then try to stay active by taking notes, sipping on a drink or asking questions. If you mess up a report because you didn't double check your work then don't get mad at yourself; use this mistake to make the next report better. Being kind to yourself allows you to keep moving forward.

> *"Success seems to be connected with action. Successful people keep moving. They make mistakes, but they don't quit."*
> - Conrad Hilton

There may be moments or days of weakness, but you should always come back to learning from your mistakes. At the end of each day, try forgiving yourself for any mistakes. Whether it is a silly comment or a major blunder, you'll notice that when you cultivate kindness for your mistakes you can use them as support for a better life.

Remember one mistake you made in the past few weeks. (There must be at least one.)

What did you learn from this mistake? (Positive and negative)

How has this mistake improved your decision making ability?

The Mirror of Difficult People

Difficult people should make us take a hard look at ourselves. Why can't we get along with a certain co-worker? Why do they make us so angry?

The answers lie within us. We need to expand our awareness past the usual answers:

- She isn't smart enough.
- He doesn't care.
- She is just a jerk.

We label someone as difficult because we don't want to invest too much emotional energy into them. We try to categorize the difficult people in our lives so we don't have to worry about what they think.

In reality we are cutting them off because we don't want to exert extra energy to deal with them. We are taking the lazy way out.

Difficult People

Peter Vajda of Slow Leadership argues that we tell ourselves stories about the people in our lives and once they are told, they become concrete. These stories are usually built on false circumstances because they are contracted versions of the truth. We create these stories because we don't want to be bothered to find out the truth. When you recognize these fake stories and learn to let go of them, you will be able to free yourself from emotional attachment.

Let's say you meet Jim, a co-worker, on the first day of your new job. He's in a bad mood and doesn't respond well to your questions. During this time, you begin to create the story and idea of what this person is like. Well the night before, Jim's wife may have told him that she wanted a divorce. If you had met Jim the day before, you would have a completely different perspective on the guy. The problem is that we keep repeating our original story in our head every time we have an interaction with that person.

The Stories We Weave

These self made stories prevent us from connecting with people who would have otherwise become a good friend or at least someone tolerable. The true nature of an individual is revealed when confronted with difficulty, whether it is a difficult person or a situation.

You can create that one story and stick with it, or you can open your awareness to the possibility that this person could help you discover more of your happiness. The more mental blocks that you can unlock, the easier difficult people and situations will become.

What is one trait of a person in your life that you struggle to accept? (e.g. He or she has an annoying laugh or gets frustrated very quickly.)

It's this trait that will teach you about your ability to be compassionate toward another person.

How could you make a little game out of enjoying this trait? (e.g. Pretend you are a sociologist trying to diagnose this person's issues)

A Project Ritual

I have always had a problem with finishing projects that I've started. My procrastination kicks in when I'm in the final stages of the project and I begin second guessing myself as well as the direction of the project.

My Ebook

I was working on an ebook to help drive more traffic to my website. I planned to give it away for free to the people who signed up to receive my articles in their inbox or blog aggregator.

My issue with procrastination was this: every time I sat down to do the work, I ended up checking my email or doing some blog marketing instead. That was my Achilles heel. I found it easier to just jump into this other work because it didn't require as much intensive brainpower. I've also always been afraid of failure and I'm not afraid to admit it. The ebook didn't turn out to be perfect (What ebook is?), but it was written to help spread the brilliant ideas that Google uses to encourage great work. Throughout the course of creating this ebook, I found that what really got me through was the use of rituals during my writing process.

Why Rituals?

I love rituals because they help reinforce good habits. Praying before bed sets the mood for your sleep, just like your morning routine before work helps you look and smell terrific, setting the tone for the day.

Here is my writing ritual that I use before I begin working on any writing project. It has helped me focus my energy, stay relaxed and accomplish high-quality work.

1. **Clean off desk** - (It's almost always a mess, because I'm working on various projects. Putting my stuff away is a whole different issue that we'll explore at a later date). This forces me to only focus on the task at hand.
2. **Close all open windows on my computer -** When I see other windows open, I'm inclined to do a quick email check.
3. **Put on music to fit the mood that I need to be in** – intense (Bach or Mozart), calming (Yoga style trance), or exciting (dance style). It all depends on how I feel and the mood that I want to create. The volume also varies depending on what I need to get done.
4. **Make a list of what I want to accomplish** - No time frame. When I put myself on a time frame it stresses me out. I just set my goals and try to get them done. If you need a time frame then go for it. Sometimes we need a little stress to motivate us.
5. **Do a one-minute relaxation** - I take 60 seconds to calm my mind and put myself in a mindset that encourages good work.
6. **Do a little self-coaching** - I ask myself, "How I can enjoy the work?" I think of the "present me" – actually doing the work and thinking about how I can get pleasure out of it. I also consider the "future me" – how accomplishing this task will improve my life. This keeps me motivated throughout my work.

7. **Get started** - This is where I used to hesitate, but now I just jump in because I have prepared myself for what I want to get done.

It works!

My writing (big project) ritual usually only takes 5 – 10 minutes, but it saves me an hour of procrastination. I've stopped putting big projects off to later in the day. My mind is most fresh after I wake up. By getting an early start on the big project, I can exhaust myself and then save the less intensive tasks (email) for later in the day.

This might not work for you, but try tweaking it to fit your style. Maybe you want to light a candle to signify your burning desire to get your stuff done, or maybe you want to do some push-ups to get your heart pumping. Whatever you do, I believe that a ritual encourages you and helps set the tone for your project. It sure beats being a big bully and forcing yourself to do work.

By creating your own ritual, you'll promote the right frame of mind to accomplish great work and also have fun.

Think of two short rituals you could do before you start a difficult project: (i.e. system of small events you could do to put you in the right frame of mind. Make a cup of tea and a short prayer to the universe to help guide you.)

How will this help your motivation?

Personal Leadership

You must lead your thoughts and emotions in order to achieve your desired results. When you become the leader of yourself, you direct your own happiness.

That means not letting anyone or anything dictate how you feel.

Check in with yourself before every decision. The more you practice, the easier it will become to make good decisions. Just make sure that you take the time to understand why you are leading yourself in a certain direction.

If someone asks you to do a project and your first thought is "boring," find out why. Use the Toyota method, the "5 Whys". You have to understand the root cause of the problem in order to solve an issue that you are experiencing.

If you don't want to work on a project because it feels wrong for some reason, you need to find out why so you can create a plan to better handle the situation.

Ask yourself "why" 5 times to understand your feelings:

1. Why: Because I hate working with Megan.
2. Why: Because she never listens to what I have to say.
3. Why: Because she doesn't care.
4. Why: Because she listens to other people and not me.
5. Why: Because I don't stand up for my ideas.

Personal leadership helps us improve how we interact with other people, especially difficult people.

Try listing 5 ways you can learn from someone you don't get along with. When you can understand why you feel various ways while interacting with others, you'll be able to reach your greatest potential.

1.

2.

3.

4.

5.

How can you apply one of these ideas this week? (e.g. I can learn to compliment people more often, like Max)

Internal Dialogue

You have a continual dialogue going on inside your head. The dialogue can be positive, negative, or neutral.

It's what you do with this dialogue that will determine your perspective.

You've probably seen a friend who can take almost any situation in stride. They seem to have a magical ability to roll with their problems. This talent is largely due to the way that they communicate with themselves.

I worked alongside a co-worker who could find the joy in every situation. I was amazed by her ability. During my time with her, I was at a point in my career where I was so pessimistic that I couldn't see even a sliver of joy in the work that I did. I hated every single person, task, and myself when I was at work.

I studied her, watching her ability to enjoy even the most stressful situation.

The most important reason for her emotional success was her ability to talk herself through a problem. There were times when I could hear her whispering encouraging thoughts to try to improve her mindset. It was a little weird, but it worked.

She took her inner dialogue to a new level. Instead of allowing her "self-talk" to beat herself up, she used it to find a constructive point of view. She built upon each thought, allowing her thoughts to take her to an internal place that brought her joy.

You have this ability, too. When you are in a stressful situation, watch your thoughts and see how they add to or subtract from your happiness. If you are having thoughts that subtract from your joy, then try to offset these thoughts with fresh angles that help you see the positive. I usually try to think of things for which I am grateful. This helps me stay balanced.

I was working on an important email to my boss and I was stuck on how to communicate my need to work on a new project that was coming in. I thought I was a good fit for the project. Right in the middle of my email, my internal dialogue went negative (i.e. I didn't deserve this new project and I couldn't do a good job).

The dialogue got pretty ugly.

I began to gently talk myself through the reasons why I deserved the project. I thought about how I kicked the last project's butt. I thought about how I needed this challenge. I thought about all the reasons why I could do a great job. I listed all my talents that would be a good fit with this project.

My mood and confidence turned around. I felt grateful for this "inner dialogue" skill. My confidence soared.

The most important aspect to using inner dialogue is compassion. Most of the time when you make a decision, you do it for the right reasons. It's not until afterwards that you might realize you made an error in judgment. So be kind and talk yourself through each problem. The more you do it, the more positive angles you will find.

Was your last inner dialogue during a mistake encouraging or mean? (Explain)

How did the dialogue affect your mood?

Recreate this dialogue and try to encourage yourself to learn from the mistake.

Create a more positive dialogue from this same situation:

Practice this dialogue until it feels natural. Try to use it the next time your inner dialogue starts to go negative. By having practiced positive dialogue to encourage you through the mistake you'll be able to bounce back quickly.

Don't Take Interactions Personally

I went to a therapist when I was in my mid twenties. I needed help. I was constantly frustrated by work, relationships and life in general.

My biggest struggle was relationships (personal and work). I was afraid to joke around with new friends for fear of hurting someone else's feelings. I was deathly afraid of what people thought of me. There were days when I decided to stay home instead of putting myself at risk of being judged by others.

Yep, I was a mess.

I thought that if I isolated myself from the pain that I would be happier. This only made me even more unhappy.

We all know that we shouldn't take other people's comments personally because they are just dealing with their own problems. I look at how angry and sad many people are. They never feel that they are treated fairly at work, in traffic or at home.

Most of the time, these people are signaling others to treat them unfairly. It goes back to creating positive inner dialogue. Instead of letting other people's negative comments bring you down, you need to see every interaction as an opportunity for growth.

I've learned that people who speak negatively about other people really see this trait in themselves. They only see life from their perspective. They haven't been able to expand beyond their own issues.

You can adjust your perspective on other people's negative comments by empathizing with them. You can allow them to say what is on their mind without taking it personally. By doing this, you will be taking the first step toward mastering your own emotions.

Whenever someone makes an upsetting comment about you, it helps to ask yourself, "Why do they feel this way about themselves?" You'll eventually stop putting the blame on yourself. When you stop taking everything personally, you can find ways to bring joy to your relationships without fear of what someone might say about you.

What was the last negative comment someone said to you?

What was the situation?

How can you use that negative comment to be more compassionate toward that person? (i.e., when someone refers to my actions as stupid, I may feel bad because they take such a negative view on a difficult situation.)

Remember 3 Good Things at the End of Each Day

When you take the time to remember 3 good things at the end of each day, you are training yourself to see the positive. A friend of mine, Alex Kjerulf, the Chief Happiness Officer, gave me this tip.

Many of us actually do the opposite: We look at all the upsetting things that have happened in our day, thinking that if we look over our mistakes we can avoid repeating them. This causes us to focus on the negative and beat ourselves up.

When I first started practicing the "3 Good Things" habit, I noticed a difference right away. Despite the fact that my job at the time was dragging me down, I found any tiny bit of joy that was in my day and added it to my list. By the time I was done listing three things, my mood had always picked up and I found myself looking at life from a more positive angle.

One day was so bleak that I didn't think I would make it to three, but I tried anyway.

This is what I came up with:

1. My mom made me laugh this morning because she said the word penis out of nowhere.
2. A lone moth flying in the rain. If he can persevere then so can I.
3. An apple I ate at lunch. I still love that first bite.

You can apply this habit at the end of your work day, too. This is a perfect activity for your commute home. If you work from home, then remove yourself from your home office and take five minutes to remember three good things that happened to you that day.

Name three good things that have happened in your day.

How did this short list make you feel?

How can you make this a daily habit? (e.g. Pick a time that you will do this every day. Write yourself a note until it becomes a daily habit.)

Work Will Not Always Be Fascinating

It is unrealistic to expect to feel happy at work 100% of the time. Even if you love what you do, there will always be dull paperwork or difficult co-workers. The idea is to love the work that you do so that the rest of the crap that you have to put up with is tolerable.

> *"Perhaps searching for passion is "not so bad"- but it has to be infused with a sense of realism that understands that it's not going to be there all the time. In fact, it seems like any way you look at happiness in the workplace, be it through passion, or "flow", or goal setting, or love, if we can indeed keep our sense of perspective through it all, we don't need 100% of any of it."*
> - Terry Starbucker (1)

When we expect to feel good all of the time, we hinder our chances of actually being happy. We strive for perfection, fall short, and then get pissed off that we missed our goal.

It is important to set realistic goals and strive for attainable results in order to be happy at work. Our expectations and perception of our results are always changing, and that's why it's so hard to find and keep those perfect feelings.

We must develop our ability to adapt to the present moment, whether it is something tedious like stuffing thousands of marketing bags or something groundbreaking like designing a new drug to cure a disease. Both need to be done and both have merit. The important thing is finding that merit and finding the hidden joy within each experience.

How have your expectations hindered your ability to be happy at work? (Do you want a raise, promotion or land a new client you feel you deserve?)

How can you adjust your expectations to bring more joy? (What positives have you been ignoring?)

(1) Terry Starbucker of http://www.terrystarbucker.com/2009/09/27/the-85-solution-for-happiness-at-work/

Speak Up and Take Action

You may be the most peaceful person in the world and perhaps this makes you happy, but when you aren't being treated fairly you have to speak up. Everyone deserves to be treated with respect.

Bullying at work has become an epidemic that needs to be addressed by every organization.

> *"From the data obtained, the researchers tell SINC that 14% of the respondents have confirmed having suffered situations of psychological abuse over the past six months, with 5.8% suffering frequently and the rest, 8.2%, occasionally."*
> - escience news from the article *Bullies have harassed 14 percent of workers over past 6 months*

This research was done in Spain, but bullies are in every organization.

I had a boss who loved to bully me. He would verbally abuse me. He once told me that he could have a monkey do a better job than me. There were days when I would go home and cry. I felt lost and out of options.

I hope that you never experience this situation, but if you do then please create a plan to change it and take quick action. WorkplaceBullying.org is a great place to start if you struggle with bullying in your workplace.

That may mean talking to the person who is bullying you or finding a better situation. You have options and people do want to help, but only you can take control of your happiness.

Do you have people in your work who have to get their way? What do they do?

Should you approach them about their actions or adjust your perspective? That's a tough question that only you can answer.

Ask yourself,"How does this person's actions make me feel?"

Are your feelings strong enough that you feel you should take action?

What would be the best way to approach this person? (e.g. strong, confident, sympathetic)

Pick a time and place that you can talk one on one with this person and explain how this person's actions make you feel. Ask them if they have any solutions. Let them feel a part of the answer.

Use Failure as Your Slingshot

The greatest business people, actors, politicians, athletes, and scientists all persevere through failure in their careers before they reach a high level of success. When they do reach that point, there comes a great calm. They realize that their disappointments were some of the best moments of their careers because they used them to improve on their next move.

Life is a beautiful struggle, and the great people of our history used each failure as a slingshot to create a better life. One of the greatest of them was Abraham Lincoln. His failures were numerous and would have crushed a weaker willed person.

Here is a list of Abraham Lincoln's setbacks that he experienced before he was elected as president:

- Failed in business in 1831
- Defeated for the legislature in 1832
- Failed in business again in 1834
- Ann Rutledge, the love of his life died in 1835
- Nervous breakdown in 1836
- Defeated in an election in 1838
- Defeated for Congress in 1843, 1846, and a third time in 1848
- Defeated for Senate in 1855
- Defeated for Vice President in 1856
- Defeated for Senate in 1858
- 1860 he was finally elected President!

Every living thing struggles. Famous actors struggle with the paparazzi, I struggle with my career, everyone struggles with their relationships, rich people struggle with illness, and everyone struggles with the possibility of death. Every struggle creates new places for joy. The truly great people understand that failure isn't the measure of a person, but it is what they do with that failure that determines how successful they become.

> *"It is a mistake to suppose that men succeed through success; they much oftener succeed through failures. Precept, study, advice, and example could never have taught them so well as failure has done."*
> - Samuel Smiles

Theodor Seuss Geisel, yep the one and only Dr. Seuss was rejected 27 times for his first kids book. The 28th publisher finally published his book. He has sold over 200 million copies of his books.

We don't see all the failures from the people that have come to support who they are. The work it took for them to gain the respect that they deserve.

The important thing is to learn how to use that struggle to help improve your life. That's what makes the difference between success and accepting defeat. Use your difficulties to make yourself stronger. Use your failure as a slingshot toward happiness and you'll succeed.

What is one failure that you've had to deal with?

How did it make you a stronger person?

Fear to Fuel

The things we fear are the experiences that we need the most.

I say this because the only way that I've grown in any of my jobs was when I was pushed outside my comfort zone.

Think back to the most rewarding experience at any job. I'll bet most of the time there was a lot of fear and struggle. When you overcame this struggle, the experience burned into your memory. There was so much growth that you will never forget the experience.

> *"You block your dream when you allow your fear to grow bigger than your faith."*
> - Mary Morrissey

You are blocking your ability to enjoy the present moment by feeding into your worries.

You have dreams every day. These dreams can make you happier and the world a better place. If you are afraid to make them real then you are depriving the world of your talents.

I was afraid to write this book. I didn't want to put my ideas out there only to be judged. There is always someone finding fault with the ideas of another. Every time I would sit down to write I procrastinated. I found easier tasks to do; tasks that didn't require such intense energy and, in the end, might not be viewed by the masses.

I wasn't living what I teach in this book. I was feeding my fears with more worries, creating a bigger monster than I wanted to deal with.

I love reflecting on this irony. It made me laugh and spurred me to laugh with my fear. When I stopped thinking that this book needed to be a life changing thing and started thinking about how these ideas could help people, that's when I used my fear to motivate me. I wanted to show myself that this imaginary pain wouldn't stop me from helping other people be happier at work.

You too can appreciate your fear and use it to motivate you. If you are worried about what your boss or a coworker may think of an idea, sit back and be with this fear. Know that you are the one creating this feeling, and only you can use it to your advantage.

What do you fear at your job? (e.g. your boss, difficult clients, public speaking)

How can you use this fear to help you grow at work?

How can you work with this fear to help you become more confident?

Using your fear to fuel your growth you are developing confidence that will help you at every level of business.

Project You Should Either Release or Keep Pursuing

Almost every detailed task, topic, or report is harder than it initially exposes itself to be. It always takes more time and more effort than expected. This happens because our thoughts are fluid. We imagine ourselves working hard and everything magically coming together, when in reality we come across many obstacles that suck away our energy and creativity.

Our imaginations are what fool us into trying for the impossible. No one wants to be viewed as a fool. We look at those first couple of weeks of American Idol and we wonder why most of them even try. They wait in line for hours only to be laughed at.

By understanding our superpowers and weaknesses, we can maximize our success. Do those awful singers really know how bad they are? I believe that most of them are fooled by what they want to see. They only listen to the people who praise every note they sing. They are tricking themselves into believing their talent will take them to great fame and fortune.

It's Easier to Believe a Dream than the Truth

If we are going to love what we do and make a living at it, we need to understand which choices are real dead ends and which look like dead ends. We must separate the impossible illusions from achievable reality in order to make success easier. This concept has been a thorn in many people's sides. We'll explore why many of us, me included, keep failing and trying something new over and over again, but never break through to real success. We will then learn how to avoid this trap and excel at what we love to do.

Where is Your Motivation?

Everyone fails, whether it is your hard working father or Bill Gates. They fail in small ways every day, but successful people put their failures behind them and try a little harder the next day. They know that there is a learning curve to every new thing. The smarter they work, the more successful they become. They are able to align their talents with their passions.

Let's say you tried to write a book. If you are like most new writers, you probably started one and never finished it. If writing isn't your thing you can substitute a book with some other very difficult creative project. You probably had a brilliant idea and got all excited. Then you hit your first wall of bricks. You smashed down the wall and kept at it. Then you came to the second wall which felt like a wall of stone. You tried crawling around it, then over it, then through it. Then you put the project aside and never came back to it.

If you ever tried writing a novel, your motivation probably got stuck when trying to tie the character's first adventure into the next. The scene became a story and you had to account for character synthesis, plot, and story line. *This happened to me*. The difficulty level increases exponentially. This is a common problem. Then you try to get yourself to sit back down and continue writing, but you just never can find the desire to make it happen. Maybe it's a significant other or another grand project that demands your attention. Whatever it is, that initial excitement fades.

When you finally have some time to really think about the book you wanted to write, you decide your time is better spent somewhere else. Maybe it's that good book that you always wanted to read or the fear of getting stuck again that distracts you from your initial burst of creative energy. It doesn't matter. You made a conscious decision to fail because the project wasn't worth your time.

How To Let Go Of Your Expectations

Failure is such a harsh word, so we'll call it a release. You released that project because the motivation was gone. This is a good thing. I've started hundreds of projects in my life and probably finished 10% of them. Not every project should be finished; actually most should be released. If you are anything like me (ADD gifted) you probably have many interests, and although it's fun to dabble, usually when a project gets more difficult it pushes you to give up.

Most of us couldn't fathom training to climb Mount Everest for a year or two then taking the risk to reach the summit. Why would someone do this?

It doesn't pay out gobs of money; in fact it costs a lot of money and time to make it all happen. I believe a person does this for two main reasons.

1. They want to challenge themselves in a way that will help them understand who they are.
2. Social status – If I'm honest and understand that it's okay to appease the ego for the right reasons then I admit that it probably does feel good to tell people the story of climbing one of the most treacherous mountains in the world.

When we push ourselves past our comfort threshold we become stronger. This can lead to happiness. Not because of the obvious accomplishment, reaching the peak, but because it changes our outlook. We see life differently after we write a book or climb Mount Everest. It gives us a glimpse into our greatness. We all know that we are great, but we don't believe it until we do something so difficult and exciting that it changes us forever. The problem that occurs when we fail is that our ego takes a hit. We become afraid.

Fear dictates our future choices. We don't want to be perceived as the William Hung (American Idol reject) of what we love to do. We want to succeed. We want to succeed so bad that it holds us down. The difficult part is in understanding when to let go and when to dig deeper and go for it all.

3 Questions You Must Ask Yourself to Understand When to Let Go or Push Through

I designed a three question process to help you understand your fear, release it, and make the smart decision to either continue with the project, or let it go and try something else. First you must find a quiet place to be with your thoughts. Then, ask yourself:

1. **"Why am I really doing this?"**

We fool ourselves into thinking that we are doing something because we want to accomplish an audacious goal, but in reality we may be doing it for someone else. You may want to impress someone you are attracted to or to prove to your parents that they didn't waste money on an art degree. You have to do some soul searching and make sure that you really want to accomplish this goal. If you do, then move on to step 2. If even the thought of continuing the project makes you cringe then don't even think another second about it, just release it; it's not worth your time. Down deep you know that it isn't in your best interest to tackle the project.

2. "Am I excited?"

Are you working on your project because it gets that little spot in your gut excited, or are you doing it because you have to? When you can honestly answer that it feels good then you can move on to step 3. If you aren't excited about the project then there is no reason to stick with it, but be careful. Don't throw away two years of work because you are in a grumpy mood. Let these thoughts settle, talk to a close friend or family member, and if the excitement is still gone then release it.

3. "How does this project fit into the future me?"

Part A: This is the last step that most people leave off. Let's use the novel example. You may want to write a book, but are you doing it because you have something to say or are you doing it because you want the results of having a published book? More than 90% of books that are published each year fail in the publishers' eyes because they don't make enough money to cover the cost of printing and marketing the book, but it won't be a failure to the writer who has larger plans. *I couldn't remember where I found this statistic, so take it for what it's worth.* He knows that it will take work to market this book and he does it because he wants to bring his ideas to others. He knows it takes years to build an audience, and he isn't going anywhere any time soon so he may as well work his butt off to get that book up and running. The hard work fits into his goal for his future.

Part B: If you are doing the work for someone else, you may not like it but you must ask yourself, "Is this helping the 'future me'?" So when your boss asks you to do a certain project, do you usually feel appreciated after it's complete and do you also feel like it will help your career? If the answer is "yes," then that's great, but if you are doing it all for the paycheck then maybe it's time to drop that dead end project (even if you are making decent money) or at least find a way to renegotiate your job duties.

Part C: If you only enjoy working on a certain project every now and again, then it's only a hobby. The stress won't overwhelm you. The desire to work on this project isn't incredibly powerful and you may go weeks without working on it, but you can enjoy each bit of progress that you create because you are doing it to relax your thoughts. It fits into the "future you" because you want to create in a "stress free" state of mind.

No project, relationship, or challenge can be considered a failure if it helps the person improve his/her life in some way. I'm on my fourth book and in some people's eyes my past projects might be failures. They aren't published, and in many writers' expectations that's a failure, but to me they are stepping stones to a smarter and stronger me. I'm building my talents in order to bring value to people's lives.

You need to work on projects that will bring a smarter and stronger you into the present. The more you try and fail, the stronger you'll get. The more you try and succeed, the smarter you'll get. You put both of those traits together and you'll be building a successful career that's going to make you happy.

What project have you worked on in the past that has felt like a failure?

Why were you really working on this project?"

Were you really excited?

How did this project fit into the future you?

Understanding past motives will help you make better choices in the future that are more closely aligned to your needs.

Dealing with Anxiety at Work

A few years ago when I was walking into an old company's building, an unsettling feeling hit my stomach. I didn't realize that I was feeling this way until right before I walked inside. How long was this feeling in me? Had I been ignoring it since last night or maybe all month?

For most of us, anxiety plays a daily role in our lives. We worry about project deadlines, co-worker relationships and what our boss thinks of us.

It's natural, but very unsettling.

Most of you are probably thinking that I'm going to give you tips on how to relax and relieve stress.

Nope.

I'm not going to regurgitate some facts about taking breaks and drinking less coffee. You all know the basics. You probably struggle with these techniques because your feelings have more control than your rational mind, which isn't a bad thing. But you do need to create a balance between rational thinking and your feelings.

No one can argue with feelings.

Feelings are there to help us make smart decisions. If we're not careful, these feelings can snowball and take over. Sometimes we may feel like we can't release them, and all we can do is suffer through them.

Whaaaat? Heck no. We all struggle, but constant struggle over the same thing is torture and also bad for your health.

What to do?

You can harness the energy created by these anxious feelings and use it to focus on the positive possibilities, rather than focusing on fear. You really can use this anxiety to build the career that makes you happy.

I'll give you a step by step plan that worked for me. I harnessed a lot of my anxiety, which has made me happier and more productive.

1. Communicate with Your Anxiety Bubbles

My anxiety usually comes from my inability to align my own needs with the goals that someone else gave me. It's a lot easier to match up your own goals with your needs, but not so easy when someone else sets the goals - especially if you don't agree with them.

Let's say your boss wants you to start a new project or maybe s/he even wants to promote you. Even if you may not have asked for this "honor," you may not be in a position to deny your boss. So you are thrust into these new duties without even wanting them.

Every time you think about these changes, anxiety bubbles up. Who should you complain to first? Yourself.

You need to find a way to communicate with your anxiety so it doesn't take over.

I make a list of ideas that help me open up to my anxiety and understand why it's there:
- Take a break to just sit and breathe.
- Let yourself feel anxiety then think of the image that is causing you to feel this way and imagine yourself breathing it out like a big balloon. Watch it float away.
- Hold your anxiety in your arms like a big baby and coddle it until it falls asleep.
- Draw your anxiety on toilet paper and flush it down the toilet.
- Pretend your anxiety is an old friend and really listen to his/her needs.

A little self understanding can go a long way to ease those fears. You need to accept your feelings; wanting to change them will only entrench the feelings even more. Talk to yourself. Allow your feelings to be there. Try to see them as a chance to learn more about yourself and your choices.

2. Get Creative

It's time to stop the cyclical thinking and get a little creative with your ideas. The goal is to find a way to align these changes in your life with your personal needs.

You need to pull yourself away from your roller coaster of emotions. Look at the facts and brainstorm a list of creative ways that this change might benefit you in order to help yourself find a better perspective.

Try coming up with as many practical perspectives as you can in fifteen minutes. (Putting a time frame on it can help you focus).

Letting your creative side loose will allow you to find a new solution that can help you release your stress.

Test out some of Your Practical Ideas:

Now you have a list of ideas. Start testing them.

My list of "practical perspectives" on a new project assignment went something like this:

- It's a chance to improve my skills.
- I get to work with Brian (cool guy).
- I can add this to my resume.
- Drawing out a mind-map will help me get my thoughts in order.
- This is an opportunity to interact with more co-workers.
- I can ask for a raise when I'm done.
- I'll get a good chance to make people laugh.
- This will inspire great ideas for Work Happy Now.
- During this project, I will watch my emotional states and how they fluctuate.

- This will help me improve my patience – every project requires developing new techniques to stay patient.
- This project will give me the opportunity to laugh more.
- I'm going to meditate before bed every night while working on this new project. (Just focusing on relieving my stress)

I was trying to align my personal needs with this new project. Of course, I resisted at first. After all, I was comfortable doing my regular routine. These new goals gave me emotional anchors.

3. Practice Every Single Day

As I began to self talk myself through my various goals, I decided that three of them would work well.

- This will inspire great ideas for Work Happy Now.
- It's a chance to improve my skills.
- I'm going to meditate every night for 10 minutes while working on this new project. (Just focusing on relieving my stress)

Every time I got down on the project, myself, or my co-workers, I began to list ways in which the project was helping me.

It was helping me with Work Happy Now by giving me plenty of ideas for articles. I wrote an article about the value of patience and a post about seeing things as they are and not as I want them to be.

As for improving my skills...

I learned to be a little more organized. I was becoming lazy and I had stopped using my calendar to keep track of meetings and deadlines. I didn't have that option anymore. Ever since that project, I've been proactively staying on top of my work.

As for meditating before bed...

I practiced Transcendental Meditation before bed. I focused on my breath and staying in the present moment. When my thoughts drifted I just brought them back to my breath. I noticed I was more calm and relaxed before bed. When I awoke my anxiety was significantly reduced and I didn't feel as nervous walking into my work.

What anxiety do you have at work?

What are three creative solutions to dealing with your anxiety? (e.g., talking to it like it's a friend, daily laughter sessions, drawing a cartoon of your anxiety)

Try each creative solution and see which one works best then apply this solution for the next 30 days to see how you feel.

When you encourage yourself to use new skills to adapt to a situation, you can create long-lasting habits. It will become easy to stick with these new habits once you discover how much they help ease your anxiety.

Measuring Your Work Happiness

How does a person measure his happiness? One day he is healthy and feeling good, then, boom, he has the flu or even a life threatening sickness and he is miserable. One of the major differences between a happy person and a grumpy person is how that person adapts to change.

I was curious to know how I adapted to my daily problems, so I checked in with myself three times a day. I tried to be as honest as I could. The weird part about this experiment was that after I would rate my happiness each time, I would think about changing the number to make it a little higher. I wanted to believe that I was always happy.

I'm not. What I learned was that each day was fascinating to me. I became more excited about my curiosity than how high my happiness score could be.

I kept track of my mood in the morning, afternoon, and night. I figured a sampling of all the major chunks of the day would be the best way to determine what patterns existed.

Here are my results:

Date	Morning	Afternoon	Night	Average	One Thought (Be specific)
7/13/2009	8	7	6	7.00	I did not complain about the Texas heat.
7/14/2009	7	6	6	6.33	I relaxed during tedious work.
7/15/2009	9	6	5	6.67	I laughed more than yesterday.
7/16/2009	7	8	9	8.00	I took 15 minutes to practice Yoga.
7/17/2009	10	5	9	8.00	I enjoyed a 100 degree heat walk.
7/18/2009	5	6	7	6.00	I made a good joke that made the whole room laugh.
7/19/2009	6	7	8	7.00	I drank too much and took a while to recover.
7/20/2009	9	9	6	8.00	I had a great cup of morning tea then began to dread Monday.
7/21/2009	8	7	7	7.33	I stayed focused on a project for three hours. I stopped pushing to finish and just relaxed with the work.
7/22/2009	4	8	8	6.67	Rolling with my mood. My stomach hurt, but it did not matter how I felt physically. I was still happy.
7/23/2009	1	3	1	1.67	Stomach Virus - glad to own a comfy couch.

7/24/2009	4	3	2	3.00	I relaxed with the pain, then rebelled, then relaxed. This happened all day long. Very exhausting.
7/25/2009	5	4	3	4.00	First day of hope after stomach flu.
7/26/2009	6	6	4	5.33	On the mend.
7/27/2009	6	7	7	6.67	Feeling healthy again.
7/28/2009	9	10	7	8.67	I loved my sandwich at lunch. I could finally enjoy food again.
7/29/2009	8	8	10	8.67	My first child was born at 4:35pm. Back to full health just in time.
7/30/2009	10	10	9	9.67	Afterglow of first child.
7/31/2009	8	8	9	8.33	We brought the baby home.
8/1/2009	8	8	8	8.00	I took care of my wife and baby.
8/2/2009	9	8	8	8.33	I love holding my child in my arms.
8/3/2009	6	7	6	6.33	First day back to work after first child. A tough adjustment.
8/4/2009	7	6	5	6.00	Fatigue setting in.
8/5/2009	4	7	7	6.00	Sleep is very important to my happiness.
8/6/2009	7	7	8	7.33	I finished a big report.
8/7/2009	8	9	6	7.67	I took the day off to be with my wife and baby.
8/8/2009	7	7	9	7.67	I finished the eCourse for Work Happy Now while the baby slept.
8/9/2009	4	5	6	5.00	I wished I was further ahead in my career.
8/10/2009	6	7	6	6.33	Watching my mood on a daily basis is an eye opener. Mood isn't as big of a happiness indicator as I thought it would be. It fluctuates too much.
8/11/2009	5	7	6	6.00	Sleep deprivation makes me very curious. My thoughts are more negative. It's an interesting result.
8/12/2009	7	6	8	7.00	I walked the dog at night and focused my energy on enjoying her.

I averaged a 6.73 over the month that I kept track of my mood. This was also with the worst stomach flu of my life. I know that the old me would have struggled to mentally bounce back as quickly as I did from the tough situations I had to deal with.

The present me realizes that feeling great isn't the only factor of happiness. Being curious about what I was doing each day made even the low mood days still interesting. When I look back on the month, I loved every experience. My mood fluctuated, but my ability to enjoy the fluctuations is getting better. If I had to rate my happiness now I would say that this month was at least a 9.3. Being there for my wife while she birthed our first child was amazing.

I know that I can enjoy more of my every day struggles. I'm looking forward to the continual process.

How would you rate your happiness right now? (Actually write a number) Why did you pick this number?

Try keeping track of your moods over the course of a month. You'll be shocked by how you will look back on a difficult time with fondness.

Spirituality and Prayer at Work

I've been thinking about what role beliefs play in my working life. It's a lot easier to feel connected to God, the universe, or whatever beliefs a person has when they are in a place of worship. But when we are at work a lot of us check our beliefs at the door. We think and react differently than we would outside of work.

One day, I was having a particularly difficult day at work. I made a mistake on a report and I couldn't find an important document that I knew I had saved. I was flipping out inside. I actually went to my car to scream. I thought I was going to have a breakdown. This was the peak of a whole bunch of other stuff that had gone wrong. A good friend was leaving work for another job, my boss had yelled at me because he didn't like my last report, and my date canceled our dinner plans for Friday. I tried to go back into my normal routine, but my heart wasn't in it.

I couldn't handle my life.

I decided that the universe needed to take some of my burdens. I went to the bathroom, locked the door, knelt down in front of the sink, placed my elbows on the counter, clasped my hands and prayed.

> Dear Work Gods,
>
> I know I'm not perfect,
> but it's hard to forgive myself for these mistakes.
>
> What I need from you is a little compassion.
>
> Please take my fears
> and worries
> and hold on to them for a little while.
>
> Give them a hug from your ever loving arms or whatever you have
> and squeeze them until they release their
> hold on me.
>
> I appreciate your help.
>
> Love,
> Karl

After giving this bathroom prayer in a soft whisper so no one could hear even if they were standing outside the bathroom door, I felt a lot better. The pain was no longer just mine; it was the Universe's too.

Next time you are in a tough spot at work, try saying a little work prayer and see how it makes you feel.

Create your own prayer for a situation at work with which you recently struggled: (Write your prayer below)

Use your prayer the next time you are in a tough situation.

Relationships

First we dealt with the control center, now it's time to get to the heart of work happiness. The relationships you build with other people all stem from the relationship that you have with yourself. If you are emotionally balanced, you will also attract like-minded people with this trait.

The people with whom you interact have their own reasons for wanting to be around you. There is no way to tell what those reasons really are. So, instead of worrying about the "why," focus on giving your superpowers/talents to the relationship.

When you give what you can when you can, the relationship will almost always be engaging, productive and a learning experience. It's when a person holds back that they are tentative and the people they are with hold back as well.

Build Friendships the Right Way

You have to be yourself from the start. If you enjoy watching dragon flies mate then don't pretend otherwise. That sentence was a little extreme for a reason - because we are all a little weird in one way or another. Think about everyone you know. They all have their quirks - that's what allows them to anchor into your heart. By accepting their uniqueness, you will set the tone for accepting them too.

When we lie, it creates a foundation that will crumble. I know you know this, yet you probably hide your true self from your co-workers/clients.

I've been guilty of trying to fit in and not being myself. I've told jokes that I didn't think were funny in order to make my co-workers laugh. Every one of them bombed. I wasn't being true to myself.

I enjoy a drink every now and again, but I know that when I have too many, I act like a jerk. I've learned to have my fun and then end it early.

An old group of co-workers used to enjoy a regular Friday happy hour that usually got out of control--nothing like breaking into cars or anything; just very loud and obnoxious conversations. I would join in and take it too far. One night we were playing a game of pool at the local bar. I painted my cheeks, forehead, and arms with the blue chalk then jumped up on the pool table, howling at the ceiling. Everyone loved it.

The hard part was that they expected this every time. This wasn't the real me. I did it to impress them. So every time we went out after that, they expected a show. I was always encouraged to do something similar, but I never did. I didn't want to be someone that I wasn't for their amusement.

The foundation was set and I couldn't change it.

You have to be yourself from the start. If you build a relationship on something that you aren't then it's doomed to fail.

Don't be afraid to talk about the real you because it's this stuff that people will remember and that will probably lead them to find a connection that makes the relationship stronger.

What part of your personality have you hidden from your co-workers? (If you enjoy eating rats for dinner please keep that to yourself, but if you enjoy reading books about martial arts, don't hold back. People want to learn about things you are interested in. Sharing the things that excite you will encourage people to share things that excite them.)

What is one quirk of a co-worker or client that you can learn to accept?

What part of your personality have you hidden from your co-workers?

How can you feel more confident letting the "real you" out for everyone to enjoy?

You have to appreciate who you are and expect other people to do the same. If they can't find reasons to appreciate you, then it's their fault for not trying hard enough.

Interactions

The quality of your interactions will determine what you can extract from your work life. If you feel calm and joyful, you'll spread that feeling to the people around you. Once you make people feel good, they will want to help you improve your life.

It's the Karma of working happy.

What you want from other people is what you should give to them.

What could you do to give more of what you want out of life? (e.g. laugh more, give more compliments, share more, etc.)

How to Change Your Company's Office Culture

My wife discovered a story about a teacher who changed her work culture with a simple plan that anyone can implement at their organization. Her work environment went from back stabbing haters to appreciative givers in a few short months.

A teacher (still no one knows her name) didn't like how the other teachers and administration treated each other. Staff gatherings were filled with fighting, politics and fear. No one seemed to even tolerate each other. This one person decided to take matters into her own hands.

She created an Appreciation Program

- She would leave a note for a co-worker and tell them how much she enjoyed working with them.
- She left candy bars with a note.
- Little stuffed bears with a note.

The most important part was the note. Each note described, in a few sentences, what she liked about the person.

No one could figure out who the person was because she threw everyone off the trail by also giving herself a present. Everyone received presents and the mystery continued. As people were trying to figure out who the generous person was, the culture began to shift. People started treating each other better. You can't treat someone with disdain when they might be the person giving you gifts and inspiring notes. Other teachers and administrative staff began to copy this teacher. They too left little gifts and notes for each other. They wanted to repay the kindness.

Silent Love

This person never came out and took credit because it would have wrecked everything she accomplished. She let everyone believe that it might be one of their friends. It could have been anyone and the mystery added to the love that built friendships at the school.

You Can, Too

If your work environment is dreary and needs a shock of love to get it happy again, then try this for yourself. Just start giving small little gifts, under $2 and a little note. Just sit back and watch what happens.

Would you ever try something like this at your company?

What type of program could you create to help improve the culture?

How could you implement this program in your organization?

How You Are Silently Signaling Your Co-workers to Treat You

It could be a look or how you walk into a room. Your co-workers have been trained to recognize these signals and treat you accordingly. We learn these social cues at a young age.

It's hard to break these habits. We can't walk around with a friend who is willing to hold a giant mirror so we can see how we look in every situation.

What can I do? I want my co-workers to like me and treat me with respect.

I used two easy tricks that worked well for me. I was not a naturally outgoing person who wanted to enter the room with a bang. You may be shy too, but you can learn to adjust your body signals so that people like and respect you. You'll be giving me silent thanks when your co-workers start smiling when you walk in the room.

1. Treat Everyone like Family (the family members you love)

The best way to be liked is to like others. I know that we've all heard this, but it's true. When you walk into the room, think of the people in the room as family and know that they love you even if they don't show it.

When I stopped worrying about what people at work thought of me, I just treated everyone like they were a brother or sister. If they did something stupid, I laughed. If I did something stupid, I laughed at myself. Family members are meant to share in misery and victory. So allow these people into your life. You may not want to talk to them about your latest ailment and what the doctor is doing for you, but share your feelings with them. Let them know what is going on in your life, as this signals them to let you know what is going on in their lives.

Make sure you start slowly when you become friendlier to your co-workers. The best way is not to start right off talking about yourself; instead, it's better to begin by listening to them. People want to be around great listeners because they can do all the talking. You've noticed how most people just want to tell you about their lives. Let them do it, and the next time you see them ask how their son, daughter, or whatever they talked about is doing. You've just made a friend for life.

Getting people to like you is not that hard. Make sure that they know you like them first. People don't want to put themselves out there and get burned, but now you know better. The best way to make friends is to give 60% and only expect 40% back. This works in any relationship, whether it is personal or business related.

When you treat everyone as family, your body signals should change. When you love someone, you are more confident and willing to approach them. You aren't afraid of what they think because you have the family connection.

2. Retrain How They View You

I'm a man of average height: 5' 10" with shoes on. I have soft brown eyes and a pleasant demeanor. This doesn't command respect in most organizations, so I have to work for it.

You can retrain how a person views you by showing them how you want to be treated. This can be hard for the shy person because it means you have to be assertive. It's very simple. If you walk into a room and someone tries to intimidate you with a loud voice, you do your best to mirror their response. It's easy to write, but hard to implement.

You can practice this by actually having a workshop at home with friends and family. Hold a workshop at home? Are you crazy? Well, if you want to put it that way then yes. I want you to practice with people whom you trust. The only way you will be able to set the tone of an interaction is by practicing.

Try to explain what is happening at work and role-play with a friend until you have it down. Then when you go into work, try relaxing and just having fun with the person as you respond back.

The world often will laugh with you if you are laughing. Most people want you to reciprocate the greeting that they've given you. If they are excited to see you, let them know you appreciate it with an excited greeting back. This will gain you respect because it shows that you aren't afraid of that person. People can sense fear by the way you position your body. So by mimicking their reaction, you are telling them that you belong on their level.

I had trouble with bullying at work a few years ago. The group picking on me wouldn't have called it bullying, but it was and it bothered me. They made fun of me in a little brother sort of way, laughing at my clothes or a comment I made. I would get upset and just wait for them to get tired and stop teasing me. One time I blew up and let them know that they were going too far. They stopped for a little while, but eventually their old habits came back, so I tried a new tactic. I began to laugh with them, joining in on making fun of me. I never put myself down, but was always willing to laugh at myself. They understood this type of behavior and began treating me as a friend. You can't take things too personally at work; otherwise your thin skin will bleed. You'll slowly get angrier and work will only get worse.

Please don't try to change your personality. You need to be yourself, but following the social rules at your work will help you get the respect that you deserve.

Love and Respect at Work

You deserve to have a great working environment, and one of the greatest skills you can learn is emotional intelligence. People with a high EQ are the ones who make friends and enjoy their jobs.

Improving your EQ is easy when you take baby steps. Most people don't come out of college with a high EQ; it's something they slowly develop through the years. Next time you feel like you aren't getting the love and respect that you deserve, try to give other people the love that they need or use the mirroring technique. Your EQ will jump a few points, making working life just a little more enjoyable.

What is your greatest emotional strength? Mine would probably be the ability to see situations from multiple angles. Responding to this question is not about being conceited; it's about understanding who you are at work and how to maximize your potential.

What makes you good at what you do?

What silent signals do you put out to your co-workers/clients?

Ask your co-workers/clients what signals you put out to them (i.e. what do you think of when you think of me?). I know this isn't easy, but you will receive great feedback.

Compare your view of yourself with the perspective of your co-workers/clients. Then figure out a way to put out the signals that will create the kind of emotions that you would like your friends, co-workers, and clients to experience.

Your Only Competition is You

"Competition is a poison to the real prize. Your real prize is reaching your goals, your short term and your long term successes. Spending time thinking about how others are unfairly beating you takes your strength away."
- Chris Brogan

Don't compare yourself to other co-workers. The more you want to be like someone else, the further you stray from your own happiness.

If you want to succeed, you have to measure against yourself. Maybe you had a goal of earning a certain amount of money in two years and you haven't done it. Why not? And how can you adjust so that you can achieve your desired results?

I made the mistake of comparing myself to others. Why wasn't I appreciated like Tom? Why didn't I make as much money as Amy?

One day I gave in to my frustration and just blurted out to Tom, "How do you do it?" He looked at me and said, "I care."

That's it.

He didn't care about what anyone else thought besides the people he dealt with. He wanted them to trust him. He worked hard to make sure that they did.

I hate to say this because I look back on this with embarrassment, but I used to bad mouth him to my friends. I wanted to tear him down just a little bit. I wanted other people to view me like they viewed him. This only took me further away from my goal. People saw my jealousy and treated me with less respect.

I should have been measuring against myself.

If I wanted more money or respect, how was I going to obtain it?

The only person you can control is yourself. I realized that I was in the wrong business and I left the company. I wasn't willing to do what it took to succeed there.

Now I'm doing what makes me happy and I'm much more successful. I get excited about adjusting my mistakes.

So measure where you are now and then create a six-month and/or one-year plan to put yourself in your desired position. By doing this, you are working on yourself (what you can control) and letting other people flourish. When you stop seeing other co-workers as competition, you can add them to your network of people who can help you.

When you look outside of yourself to measure your success, you get lost in jealousy. Focus on what you can do and you'll improve more rapidly and have fun doing it.

Who do you measure yourself against?

Instead of thinking of this person as competition, how can you use this desire and turn it into motivation to measure your own success? (e.g. I want to drive a car like Mark. I want a car like Mark because he can afford it.) Now figure out what you want to earn and come up with a plan to make that desire come true. If you want to do this in one year, double that amount of time to two years. Check in and see where you are after one year and decide what you need to do to adjust to your goal.

Note: Successful people will tell you that it's not the car that made them happy; it's how they reached their goal to buy the car that mattered.

Note 2: You can admire traits within someone that you can learn from. This of course is different from feeling jealousy. Maybe someone you know is effective at managing their work flow you may want to ask them how they do it so you can improve your skills.

Be a Co-worker Who Gives Energy

We are surrounded by energy suckers and givers. What category do you put yourself in? It's probably an energy giver. No one wants to think of themselves as an energy sucker.

Let me ask you this...Do you complain at work? Yes? Most of us do and sometimes it's good, but there is a thin line of overdoing it. You can tell when you are overdoing it when people aren't complaining with you.

Next time you are complaining about your boss or about a certain project then take notice if people are joining in. If they are silent then you may be an energy drainer. Once you are labeled an energy drainer by your peers, it's going to take a lot of work to overcome this stigma.

Most of us want to be energy givers because these are the people who pick us up when we are down. We also want to be around these people because they make us feel good about ourselves. You can become a giver by cutting back on your complaining and putting your energy toward encouraging others.

As soon as a complaint floats into your mind, try holding it in and doing a mental 180 by giving a compliment or some encouragement to someone around you instead. When you do this over an extended period of time, people will want to work with you. You'll create a happier work environment by giving people positive feelings.

What was a recent gathering where you complained?

How could you have acted differently?

How could you apply this change in a similar situation?

15 Simple and Easy Compliments to Give Your Co-workers

My wife and I were discussing the need for people to compliment each other at work. Not enough of us give out compliments on a regular basis.

We all love it, but don't practice it. We get too caught up in our own business and forget to thank the people who help make our job easier, fun or more creative.

I've put together a list of 15 compliments that you could use at your job. They will need to be adapted for your situation, but that shouldn't be too difficult.

1. "Thank you for helping me with (insert project here). I couldn't have done it without you."
2. "You are awesome because (insert thing they do well here)."
3. After a co-worker did something to help you or the company, "What would we do without you?"
4. "You're such a good friend." (Only say this to a good friend, of course.)
5. "I love it when you save me from (insert mistake here)."
6. "I never would have thought of that. Thank you."
7. "Wow, your mind is amazing!"
8. "If I could buy you a full page ad in the newspaper touting your skills, I would." (This might be a bit much, but I know that I would love to hear that one from my boss.)
9. "I appreciate your hard work."
10. "You deserve co-worker of the year."
11. "Thanks for chipping in on (insert task here)."
12. "You are too much. You always go above and beyond."
13. "When are you going to stop making me look bad?" (Give a nudge and a laugh with this one.)
14. "You've taught me so much. I appreciate your willingness to help me."
15. "Can you teach me how to do that?" (People love to hear that they have a skill that you want to learn).

List three people whom you can compliment at work:

Create a compliment for each person:

Find a way to give those three people a compliment over the next week.

* After I gave out three compliments I noticed that these three people were more willing to smile at me. I also asked one for a favor and she was more than happy to oblige. Complimenting people is one of the best ways to build friendships. Most people want to feel loved, so you are helping fill this need. To do this well you must be honest and sincere, otherwise you won't have the desired effect.

Listen to Your Co-workers

A co-worker of mine flew to California for a funeral. Her sister, who was 74, died due to many complications. When she arrived back at work I greeted her and asked,

"Was it sad?"

"Well, yeah," she responded.

"Oh, Karl. You need to work on your social skills," responded another co-worker from the cubicle next to us.

"What I was trying to ask was…She was having complications, sometimes it's better to have them pass on than suffer through a painful life."

"It wasn't all sad. It was nice to see my family."

"See," I blurted out at the other co-worker.

It was too late. I had asked a compassionate question in the wrong way. My first reaction was to get upset at the other co-worker who butted in on our conversation. As I went back to my desk, I started replaying the situation.

The other co-worker was right. Of course it was sad; if she would have said otherwise she would have been perceived as callous. I should have asked the question that I really wanted to ask.

"How was your trip?"

Then I would have been given a story about how nice it was to see her other sisters.

If I would have just listened to my co-worker instead of getting mad and dismissing his snide remark, I would have learned a little something. I need to ask the questions that are really on my mind instead of asking some lame question that I know the answer to.

We work so closely with our co-workers that they will often give us gems that we can use to improve our lives. These same gems can cause us to get upset because they may attack our ego, but if we can let go of our egos, we can use people's comments to really improve ourselves.

If I had been afraid to listen to this feedback, I wouldn't have learned how to improve my ability to ask a good question. This may seem trivial, but it's not. Every reaction, response, and interaction is a chance to improve and enjoy ourselves.

By taking a second to reflect on what information you really want to know, you can get the answers that help you improve your relationships.

By adjusting the way that you ask a question, you can really get more useful information. This may come naturally for some of you, but for those of you who often don't get the responses that you really need, try varying the way you ask questions and then take notice of the responses you get in return.

Recall a recent comment from a co-worker or client that you didn't like.

How can you adjust the way you react to an unwanted comment?

How can you use this comment to grow?

Never Stop Expanding Your Network

You may do your job well, even so well that no one can complain, but do you find that you still never get ahead? This career trap can cause many problems. The cause of the problem may be that you are one dimensional. You are so good at what you do and you've become so comfortable that you've stopped sharing thoughts, ideas, and helpful hints.

I've seen friends fall into this trap. When they need to expand their network they ignore the signs.

- Co-workers stop coming to them for help.
- They don't reach out to people below and above them.
- They don't take advantage of programs that might help them expand their skills.

Your Corporate Network

Many of you may be imagining some old man on the verge of retirement who has trouble adapting to the latest computer programs at work. However, losing touch with your corporate network can happen at any age. I'm only in my 30s, but a few months ago I felt like I had become complacent at my job and I wasn't keeping my co-worker network strong.

I decided to start calling people within the organization just to say hi. I always made it short and sweet and kept the conversation focused on them. They loved it. As a result, they have been more willing to help me out with a problem instead of pushing me on to someone else.

Customer Network

This same problem can happen with your customer base. When we get too comfortable and we stop reaching out to old contacts, we hinder the circular flow of love from our networks that helps us succeed.

You have to communicate to all levels within the organization to stay on the pulse of your company or your business, but you don't have to push from just one angle. If you sell refrigerators and all you do is talk about how good they are, all day every day, people will tune you out.

Talk to people about the topic they enjoy most – themselves. Let them remember you for your graciousness and they will return the favor.

Who would you like to add to your career network?

What can you do to expand your network?

Results

We dealt with the control center and the heart of work happiness, and now it's time to deal with how both of these can create the outcomes we are looking to achieve.

You probably would love to accomplish more, do amazing work, and feel so relaxed and happy doing it that work doesn't feel like work. It's just an opportunity to be awesome. Don't we all?

I thought that if I was tough on myself then I would get the results that I expected. The more I forced myself to do the hard stuff, the more I procrastinated. By labeling a certain task as "hard," I was more likely to avoid it. I created the pain in my head before I even performed the action.

You can create the results that you need by being kind to yourself.

Most of us struggle with procrastination. I can't think of someone who doesn't procrastinate on something. There is always more than one thing on our "to do" list.

Work should never feel forced. We may need a kind word or thought to encourage ourselves to get started, but this is natural. You need to figure out how to provide this to yourself without letting external factors kill your motivation.

Find Your Rhythm

Your ability to accomplish great results requires that you build a system that supports your actions. Once again, it all comes back to your foundation. If you focus on doing the most important stuff first, you will get the important stuff accomplished.

The problem is that we forget this simple fact. We procrastinate by surfing the web, watching TV, and purposely doing easy tasks that make us feel good, but don't get much accomplished.

I used to start my day by checking email and responding back to every inquiry. I stopped this practice because it felt like I was chasing my tail. After writing one email, I would receive two more. Now I start my day by checking my email, but I limit myself to ten minutes to make sure that there are no emergencies and then I do the important stuff. By working on the important stuff first (i.e., writing, networking, sales), I found that I got a lot more accomplished. Then as my energy wanes I answer my emails in the afternoon, use social media to promote my business, and do other easier tasks that don't require as much intensive energy.

You must find the rhythm that works best for you. Maybe it's easier for you to do the intensive work late at night, but however and whenever you do your work, make sure that you understand your rhythm so you can be productive every single day.

When do you work best? (What time of day are you most focused? It's usually a two to four hour block of time.)

Figure out a plan to use this time to do the stuff that makes you feel powerful and smart. So if you have the most energy and focus from 9am to 1pm, then make this your "I'm a super hero" time. This is time that will usually produce the best results.

Utilize Smart Breaks

Smart breaks replenish the mind and body. Without a good break between tasks, you won't be able to stay productive. You know how inefficient your brain becomes when you work too hard, whether you are studying or working on a project for hours at a time. You get cranky and start to cut corners.

The difference between a smart break and a regular leisure break is the focus. Anyone can take a break, but most breaks don't really help you release your stress and prepare you to go back to work. A smart break is an optimized break that allows you to rejuvenate yourself.

I've been guilty of not taking smart breaks. I would waste my "break time" either stressing out about the task I was working on or worrying about something else in my life. TV was a terrible habit. I would go watch TV and forget about my troubles, but then I would just go right back to them when I went back to work. I had difficulty relaxing my mind in order to replenish my creativity.

I needed to learn to relax in the moment and not let any thoughts distract me from my purpose. When I returned to work on my project and I could still feel my mind going to mush, I figured out that the best thing for me to do was just to get up and start walking somewhere, anywhere. My favorite place is outside. Nature is a great source of serenity and being out in nature replenishes my energy. I've found that a walk outside allows me to go back to work with a fresh angle on the problem.

The best part about taking smart breaks is that the more a person utilizes this stress reducer, the more it helps. It also takes less time with practice. You will eventually learn to recognize when you need a break and know exactly how to reenergize yourself back to feeling good. A few years ago, I needed 15 – 20 minutes to replenish my energy. Now I can usually recharge in 5 – 10 minutes.

Once you find out what works best for you, just keep tweaking it until it becomes a habit that you look forward to. Once smart breaks become a part of your routine, you'll find that you are more motivated and productive.

What type of break would make you feel most refreshed?

How can you improve your breaks so you actually feel relaxed when you go back to work?

How can you create a system of breaks that fit your schedule and needs? (e.g. Use an egg timer to encourage you to step away from your desk every 30 minutes, or every morning and evening you take a break at the same time)

Mindful Work

Have you ever walked into a room and forgotten what you were there to get?

It has happened to all of us.

We get lost in our thoughts. It's like we are trapped within a room with no exit. The thoughts keep turning and shifting and we keep following. There is no end.

There is an end.

Try Mindful Working

You can bring your focus back to the present moment and just be there.

The reason this helps you enjoy work more is because it takes your focus away from what you want to happen or what did happen and instead it helps you focus on what is happening right here and now. It's so much easier to enjoy what is.

Let's say I'm drinking a cup of tea (substitute coffee if it puts you a little deeper in the moment). There is the glorious smell, delicious taste, the sounds of me softly slurping and swallowing, the sight of the cup's soft blue and white design, and the feeling of the hot mug in my hands.

There are so many more sensory anchors for us to focus on that can help us find reasons to enjoy whatever we are doing. You need to find your anchors that keep you enjoying the present moment.

I found a wonderful quote that puts all of this into perspective:

> *"Whatever you do, you will be doing extraordinarily well, because the doing itself becomes the focal point of your attention. You're doing then becomes a channel through which consciousness enters this world. This means there is quality in what you do, even in the most simple action, like turning the pages in the phone book or walking across the room. The main purpose for turning the pages is to turn the pages; the secondary purpose is to find a phone number. The main purpose for walking across the room is to walk across the room; the secondary purpose is to pick up a book at the other end, and the moment you pick up the book, that becomes your main purpose."*
> - Eckhart Tolle from the book *A New Earth*

I've gotten stuck too many times in negative or small-minded thoughts that tear my happiness and confidence down. This habit has been tough for me to break. I practiced feeling the present moment instead of thinking about what I would do next. When you really watch your thoughts as you perform a task, you'll notice that you are probably thinking about a lot of other things instead of enjoying the task at hand.

So try focusing on the *main purpose* of whatever you do while you are at work. See how it makes you feel.

Watch your thoughts and feelings and try to be as honest with yourself as you can.

- When you write an email, are you completely there?
- When you talk on the phone, are you completely there?
- When you are driving home, are you completely there?

Take notice of your wandering thoughts. My thoughts often wander to a worry, which causes pain. This pain then cycles into new and undiscovered pains. The slow times at work are the worst. I am trapped with my thoughts. That's why I recommend getting to know your thoughts through active relaxation (next chapter). By taking the time to sit and just watch your thoughts for a few minutes each day, you can reduce and even eliminate this pain cycle.

Take notes of your wandering thoughts during one of your next tasks.

What do you think about while you are working?

What could you do to remind yourself to focus on the present moment?

How can you stay focused on the task you are working on?

Some tasks just won't fit your superpowers. Everyone's mind will wander while stuffing envelopes.

Notice which projects keep your focus and which ones encourage your mind to wander. The projects that keep your focus for extended periods of time are more closely aligned with your superpowers.

Active Relaxation

To eliminate your pain, you must deal with its source. It all starts with your perspective. You can't change outside influences. The only thing you can change is how you view them.

That means bringing more self awareness to your working life through active relaxation. You don't need a meditation cushion, a quiet room, or calming music. All you need is yourself, your thoughts, and your breath and you have all the ingredients that you need.

I've created a bunch of active relaxations that I use whenever I'm feeling stressed, anxious, or when I'm just trying to do a little self-discovery. The one below is one of my favorites. You should try to practice this active relaxation for at least one minute every day. Twenty minutes is optimal, but most of you don't have twenty minute chunks to use on actively relaxing. The best thing is to give yourself at least a minute. Most of us have at least 60 seconds to help ourselves feel better.

First you must understand when you must apply a relaxation. The signs are usually hard to recognize. We get so used to holding our stress in our muscles we don't even realize that we feel stressed.

My stress usually shows itself in my muscles then my thoughts. My jaw, neck, or back begin to feel tight then I begin to get depressed. When my thoughts become negative I know that I need to slow down and redirect my attitude.

Here is one of my favorites.

Frustrated as all Heck Relaxation

How:

Over exaggerate your posture and facial expression so you are conveying frustration. Feel the alignment of your neck and spine. Stay in this posture for thirty seconds. Then slowly straighten your spine and focus on relaxing your shoulders, back and legs. Stay in this posture for another thirty seconds. Repeat this process until you've released your frustration.

Focus on:

What is your perspective at this moment? What are thinking about? How is your body posture? Are you tense or slumped? How does a straightened posture feel?

When to do this Active Relaxation:

- You are stuck working late on a project.
- You can't figure out a solution to a difficult project.
- You need to reconnect with your relaxed perspective.

Why:

Your body is probably sending signals to feel frustrated. This perpetuates your negative feelings. Instead of encouraging these negative thoughts, allow your awareness to kick in and understand this posture. When your frustration kicks in, you should only accept it for a short time and then move onto a more positive posture.

Where:

- In traffic
- At your desk
- During a phone call

What I liked:

I was actually interrupted in the middle of my relaxation by my boss, asking me if everything was okay. The best part was that everything *was* okay. I was focused on bringing awareness to my frustration, which helped me release it.

Who could use this relaxation:

- VP of Operations
- Cashier for a convenience store
- Student who needs a small break from studying.

If you are interested in reading more about Active Relaxation then go to Work Happy Now. There will be a book due out soon, so check the "shop" to see if it's there.

Create your own Active Relaxation

Your How:

What should you Focus on?

When to do this Active Relaxation?

Why you like doing this Active Relaxation?

Where do you get the best results?

What you liked about the process?

Mental Boosts that Never Fail

Most people can accomplish a lot of work when they are feeling good, but being able to be productive during a lazy day is a learned skill. I know that I've struggled with my motivation, especially after being scolded for a mistake.

There is one rule that you must keep in mind:

You'll rarely ever be as productive on a low motivational day as you would on a motivated day. Accept this (stop being a big bully to yourself) and work with the attitude you have.

If you can remember this rule then you can feel successful on low motivational days. There have been days that have started slow and I've been able to get my internal motivation excited and it turns into a highly productive day, but this is rare and never seems to last the whole day through. When I work with the flow of my mind, I'm able to maximize its ability.

It doesn't matter if you work for a company, yourself, or if you're jobless; there are always days that never go quite the way you want them to. I've been refining eight mental tricks that I've used over the past couple of years to turn a low motivational day into a productive one.

Eight Mental tricks:

1. Make It a Game

I've dealt with many low motivational days and the first one that comes to mind is the day I call "Why is everyone yelling at me." I was yelled at by the President of the company for a small mistake on an important report and for missing a meeting, by a co-worker for being too pushy, by a driver who I accidentally cut off, by a lady who didn't like my dog sniffing up on her, and by my mom in an email I read before bed. I had to think of all these mistakes and realize that they are moments that I can use. Like a character in a video game or a baseball player coming out of a slump, I can learn to use my mistakes to improve my next move.

After I was yelled at for the third time, I began to see that it was mostly my mistakes that were causing my low motivation. I knew that I had to release these errors or my motivation would sink even lower. I looked at myself from the third person, as if it wasn't me getting yelled at, but just my character I was controlling that day. All this yelling couldn't hurt me if I was just a character in a game. It would only make me stronger and improve my ability to make a better decision.

2. Watch Your Emotions

Waking up and knowing that the day will be a struggle is a feeling I now revel in. The last time I awoke with low motivation I actually smiled. I saw the emotional possibility in front of me.

As I sat at my desk, I drank a cup of caffeinated tea to spark my motivation. Nothing happened. My energy level felt lower. I knew that the day was going to be a challenge. I was lucky that on this day I wouldn't need a lot of energy. I could just take my time and perform each task methodically. I felt like I was in a haze. I had to read a report four times before it finally sank in. By watching how I reacted and not trying to force myself to snap out of it, I was able to cruise through the day and get many things accomplished.

- Stuffing marketing bags
- Writing an email to a co-worker
- Setting up a few appointments
- Enjoying my lunch outside
- Reading a report and summarizing it for my boss

After the day was done, I realized that by just watching my mood and going with the feelings, I was able to be more accepting of my circumstances. I didn't push myself into a grumpier state and the day ended up being one of average productivity that was probably better than some of my more motivated days.

3. Enjoy the External Show

Sitting through a two-hour meeting is never fun, but it can be enjoyable. Although it's difficult to focus, it is possible to cajole my attention. There was a two and a half hour meeting that I got roped into because they wanted my input. The meeting was only 10% relevant to me, so I was stuck and unable to participate for most of it.

I looked at this meeting as an opportunity to study people's facial expressions. I am usually so caught up trying to express my point of view in meetings that I miss a lot of the show in front of me. This time I made sure to watch each smile, wrinkle of the eye and nervous habit. I got so into the meeting that when it ended I felt disappointed. This technique also allowed me to listen in a different way and I came away with new ideas and respect for people who I had never really given a chance before.

4. Immerse Yourself

Dive into the sand of low motivation and bury yourself and see what happens. Sometimes I have trouble getting out of the emotional weight, but this technique can work. During one particularly rough Sunday when I had to mow the grass, write a blog, clean the kitchen, and cook dinner, I immersed myself in the low motivational feelings.

I sat down on the floor and let out a large breath. I knew I could not ignore this mood, so I dove in and felt everything that was going on within me. My sluggish thoughts, the negative emotions, and the desire to close my eyes, lean back and take a nap on the floor. That's what I did. I fell into the low motivation, letting my thoughts and feelings take me where they wanted. I set a timer for twenty minutes and gave myself that time to just relax and allow the feelings to do what they wanted. After the timer woke me up, the feelings were gone and I could sense my energy rising. I was able to get all my tasks done and I also wrote two emails to a couple of friends.

5. Compromise with Yourself

When I've been stuck in a low motivational day but I still needed to get certain things done, I made sure to give myself opportunities for mental breaks throughout the day. I created a little plan to keep my motivation balanced.

8:30 – 8:45 I relaxed and drank some coffee while reading my emails.
8:45 – 10:00 I got to work on my report.
10:00 – 10:30 I went for a walk around the office and stopped by John's cubicle to talk for a little while.
10:30 – 12:00 I got back to my report and finished the first draft.
12:00 – 1:00 Lunch
1:00 – 2:30 I edited the report and finalized its content.
2:30 – 3:00 I walked around the office building and read an article about marketing that I saved on my computer.
3:00 – 4:30 I reviewed the report and sent it to my boss.
4:30 – 5:00 I coasted through the rest of the day by cleaning up my desk and talking to my wife on the phone.

Not every day can be a sprint through work; you have to compromise on those days that your body is just begging for a break. You'll be less likely to burn out.

6. Tackle the Easy Stuff

Allowing myself to work at a more compassionate pace has helped me use low motivational days to my advantage. I usually get monotonous and time draining work done, so when I am motivated to tackle the big projects I don't have to worry about tedious stuff.

Every job has its tasks that require mind numbing focus. I have to stuff marketing bags and fill in forms, jobs that any middle school student could do, but since I must listen to the boss's wishes I have to get it done. When I have low motivational days I am able to get the tedious stuff accomplished. The bonus is that I look busy and productive to my boss and I get the work done that I normally put off for later. During low motivational days I'm just not able to focus on the difficult stuff, so stuffing bags and writing emails is the best way to get through the day and then be able to relax at home.

7. Know that the Next Day Won't be as Bad

Some days are just rough on the psyche. Instead of thinking of the day as fixed in stone, I imagine myself getting tougher after each setback. I imagine that life is offering me a mental work out. I actually picture my head growing as if I was a cartoon character.

I remember one day in particular when every time I tried to work on a report I would get interrupted, or if I tried to do some research into our competition I was blocked by my company's Internet filter, or I just couldn't get the right words out to get my point across in an email. I felt like I failed at everything I tried to do. I used each stumble or failure as a stepping stone to alter my feelings. I imagined the mental drain (black ooze) leaving my brain, converting into energy (white light), and entering my muscles, storing up for the next day. I saw the next day as a highly motivated day because I had built up all this extra energy. It worked. I plunged through the rest of day. The next day was high energy and productive.

8. Give In

Sometimes there's nothing you can do; you've tried the seven mental tricks from above and you can't get out of your funk. Go with it and stop fighting your feelings.

The last time I felt like this I had some time off with pay, so I used it. I couldn't be in the office any longer, so I told my boss that I wasn't feeling well and I needed to go home. I had to take a mental health day or I was going to explode. I watched a movie that I'd been putting off for weeks and I cooked dinner for my wife. That smile on her face perked up my day and I could feel the sluggishness oozing out of myself.

Each day has its own challenges, no matter how brilliant you are. These mental tips can be applied in almost any circumstance. Give your mind a new perspective and apply one of the tips to make any low motivational day into a productive one.

How do your mood fluctuations alter your motivation?

How can you optimize these fluctuations to get the best results out of yourself?

How Transitions Can Dramatically Improve Your Productivity

You may swig down your coffee between emails, trying to get all your tasks done, but you still can't keep up with all your work. This hyper-active pace creates productivity gaps.

Instead of creating smooth transitions from one task to the next, you are probably jumping around like a caffeinated dog. *I've seen my friend's dog drunk on coffee and it isn't pretty.*

You're missing out on a vital need.

You need time to process your thoughts from the previous task to the current one. Sure you're getting your work done, but how do you feel at the end of the day? Do you feel energized to hang out with friends and family?

Our brains are sponges constantly soaking up information, but we need to take the time to squeeze it out every once in awhile (well, it really should be all the time) to keep ourselves healthy. Burn-out wastes more of company money than employee vacations. Actually, people need to take more vacations in America because we are over worked. When employees take time off, they are able to shake out the emotional crap that builds up throughout the year. When they come back to work they have new ideas that they can't wait to share with their co-workers. Well...not everyone, but the ones who enjoy their job.

Wring Out Your Brain More Often

All the information builds up, and like any memory drive it needs to be cleaned out or it can't run efficiently. When you just go, go, go until you just can't "go" any longer, then it's time to squeeze out that brain by giving it a break.

A break is always good for your health, but most of us only take short breaks in the morning and afternoon. This isn't enough. And most of the time we are so busy worrying about work that it doesn't even feel like a break. You need to take the time to process the emotional data that has built up over the past couple of hours.

If you want your breaks to actually leave you feeling refreshed, you should take small breaks between tasks. When you finish an email, give yourself 30 seconds to process and set up your next task. I usually make a mental note, but you may want to make a physical note when you first start (I'll explain in the 4-step process).

4 Step Process to More Motivation and Less Stress

Step 1: When you finish an email or another small task, then it's time to take a moment to let out a breath. By actually being aware of this "out breath," you are taking the transition by the horns. This allows you to process the email and then think of what you need to do next. When you let out the breath, softly say to yourself, "With this out breath I let go of my stress." When you breathe back in say to yourself, "With this breath I feel calm."

Step 2: Let's say you need to edit a three page report next. Lean back in your chair, get up and do a stretch or just take a moment to let your thoughts settle. If you need to look busy because you work in a cubicle (I've been there), then write down what you will do next on a little Post-it note, close your eyes for 30 seconds, looking like you are trying to remember something, to give your eyes a rest as well. This keeps you looking busy while allowing yourself to relax your mind.

Step 3: Before you dive back in to the next task I suggest a ten second inner dialog. Tell yourself what you want to accomplish in this next task and how long you expect it to take. This helps create mental leverage.

Step 4: Right before you begin the next task, notice how you feel. This last step is most important. Why? Because it reinforces the good that you do when you take time to process, relax and set yourself up for your next task. The only way to change a bad habit and replace it with a good one is to show yourself that the new habit is worth doing. If you do this four step transition process once every hour, that's only eight minutes in an eight hour workday. *We can all spare eight minutes to reduce our stress and improve our productivity.*

Results: Taking the time to transition between tasks will keep your motivation high and your brain functioning at an optimal level. This small recurring gift to yourself will allow you to relax on your breaks and during lunch. And when you get home you won't feel as tired. This is the best part. My wife has seen such a difference in my attitude; she asked me if something changed at work.

I smiled and replied, "Yep, me."

You have the ability to make work fit into your natural rhythms. It will take a little coaxing, practice, and playfulness, but believe me, once it becomes a habit you won't ever go back to rushing through your work.

What task do you have trouble transitioning into?

Walk yourself through transition steps:

1. Relax your breathing
2. Take a few moments to move around (lean back in your chair and stretch or take a walk around to stretch your legs).
3. 10 seconds on inner positive dialog
4. Before you begin the next task notice how you feel. Did the positive dialog help?

Outer Order Adds to Inner Calm

You have probably had a messy time in your life. Even the cleanest people feel like they have had a messy period in their life because they have become more orderly with age.

You have to keep things somewhat organized or things get lost, ideas never get accomplished, and stuff piles up.

I often feel scattered and lost because of my lack of organization, so when I take some time to clean up my office, I feel more relaxed. This organization makes me feel like I can focus on the task at hand.

Most of us need to create a system so we can feel more relaxed. Next time you are working on a big project, put away everything on your desk, put on relaxing music, and see how you feel. Is it easier to focus?

By noticing how your exterior environment makes you feel, you will find it easier to set the mood to do work that creates great results.

The tricky part in getting yourself organized is figuring out an emotional anchor that will get you motivated to organize your space. This emotional anchor could be picturing your clean desk or knowing that when you reach for an object it will be there instead of buried underneath a whole bunch of crap.

What could be your emotional anchor to encourage you to actually organize your work space?

What could you organize in your space to help you feel more relaxed?

What could you do to make it seem more fun to actually organize this part of your space?

Try using your idea today. Take just fifteen minutes to organize this part of your space. Notice how you feel after you are done. Did it help or hinder? How can you adjust?

You may also want to add a little color to your environment to create the type of atmosphere that encourages great work.

Red - increased energy (Too much of it could also trigger increased aggressiveness.)
Orange – creativity, attraction, success
Yellow - personal power, happiness, energy

Green - calming, trusting, healing
Bright blue - communication and expression of creativity
Indigo - introspection and intuition
Violet - spiritual
Navy Blue - authoritative - or sometimes authoritarian

Color associations were suggested by my editor, Sue.

Here are a couple of links for background info on color and meaning:

http://www.color-wheel-pro.com/color-meaning.html
http://www.threeheartscompany.com/chakra.html

What is one change you can make to splash some color and motivation into your work environment?

How do you think this color change will improve your work?

Stop Organizing and Simplify

> *"Our life is frittered away by detail ... simplify, simplify."*
> - Henry David Thoreau

I know I just talked about organizing, but sometimes we need to do more than just put stuff away. We need to simplify--not just move our crap into containers and files.

You may have fallen into the emotional trap of organizing instead of getting rid of the stuff you don't need. You probably waste a lot of hours each month trying to organize stuff that you don't need any more.

Each month you are probably...
-   Filing papers you don't need.
-   Buying programs that don't help you work more efficiently.
-   Planning out a "to do" list that never gets completely done.

This extra work can clutter up your day. You are just moving stuff around (avoiding work) instead of focusing on the really important stuff.

Here are a few rules I'm trying to live by:
1. If I haven't touched it in over a year I donate it to Goodwill or throw it away.
2. Keep only the files (computer and paper) that I will need for over a year.
3. If I come across something that I haven't used in a while I try to find a way to get rid of it.

We can only keep one thought in our head at a time. Why do we try to clutter our space with stuff that only distracts us? The more you study your work habits, the more you'll begin to appreciate that simplifying your workspace is much more conducive to accomplishing your goals.

What can you get rid of in your workspace?

Then make a mental list of why you need to get rid of this stuff because you've been holding on to this stuff for a reason. Just because you clear it out now all that means is something will replace it. That is until you develop the habit of simplifying your life and being ok with it.

You need to retrain your brain to enjoy this new freedom from attachment of things. By making a list of everything you get rid you'll be reinforcing this new you to be ok with less crap in your space so you are free to have more time to create.

What is one thing you've held on to, but haven't touched or looked at in over a year?

Why do you think you've held on to this thing?

Can you give it away or throw it away?

By understanding your attachments you can make sure not to keep falling into the same clutter trap every time you acquire something new. For example when you buy a new digital camera give the old one away. Don't just put it in a drawer and forget about it.

55 Tips to Make Work More Fun

1. Take 60 seconds to think about your favorite moment at work.
2. Invite a new co-worker out to lunch.
3. Bring an extra dessert for your boss.
4. Eat perfectly ripened grapes.
5. Watch a YouTube video – search "Office Pranks."
6. Come up with a wild idea for the advertising department, even if you aren't in their department.
7. Buy donuts for everyone.
8. Bring in orange juice for everyone.
9. Find an awesome joke online, memorize it and tell it to everyone.
10. Don't wear any underwear.
11. Bring in freshly brewed sun tea.
12. Make everyone a copy of your favorite music.
13. Have a paper airplane contest. Whoever's plane goes the farthest gets an extra 15 minute break.
14. Wear two different colored socks, and see if anyone notices. (Want to take it a step further? Try wearing two different shoes).
15. Give a friendly wink and a smile at someone that you know won't report you to HR.
16. Bake cupcakes.
17. Write a poem and print out a copy for everyone.
18. Make everyone gather for a group photo.
19. Compliment everyone that you interact with.
20. Ask everyone how they are feeling (really listen).
21. Bring in a plant for your desk.
22. Bring in stickers that a third grade teacher would have, i.e. "You are Great," and pass them out.
23. Ask all your co-workers for their best joke. The best one gets a cup of coffee or beer.
24. Create a "show and tell" every Friday.
25. Have a child paint the office a picture.
26. Stretch at your desk for five minutes.
27. Bring in your old magazines and put them in the lunch room for someone else to read.
28. Laugh at yourself.
29. Give a copy of your favorite book to the employee who annoys you the most.
30. Celebrate everyone's birthday – tailor it to their interests (note: do not buy a generic cake).
31. Dress up like it's a party.
32. Celebrate a big contract or completion of a project by having music, dancing and a prize of a dinner for two.
33. Wash a co-worker's car during your lunch.
34. Have a dress-up day on a random day (besides Halloween).
35. Switch jobs with someone in your department for a day.
36. Have a fifteen minute exercise break for the whole office.
37. Write a letter to the most famous person in your industry asking for one piece of advice.
38. Do a 1 minute relaxation exercise that makes you look weird (like yoga nostril breathing), but you don't care because you're relieving stress.
39. Have a coloring contest – it brings back the "kid in school" feeling.

40. Make a cup of hot tea for a co-worker.
41. Trade sweaters with someone of the same size.
42. Bring in a carved design in a piece of fruit (what type of fruit depends on the season).
43. Wear all white.
44. Give a small gift to all your co-workers.
45. Give every co-worker a special rock that you picked for them and tell them why they got the rock that you gave them.
46. Bring in a board game and play it during lunch.
47. Everyone write a "thank you" note to their favorite client, customer, or business.
48. Let someone borrow your favorite pen.
49. Do your boss's or co-workers' most hated task.
50. Throw a party for everyone in the office. Give one reason why you appreciate each person and that's why you are throwing a party for everyone.
51. Bring in face paints and paint employees' and customers' faces.
52. Bring in a cool piece of original art from home and display it in the office.
53. Create a company song.
54. Ask everyone what their favorite animal is and why.
55. Bring in Trivial Pursuit cards and ask people questions. If they get it right they win a piece of candy.

What could you do to make work more fun? (List 5 things)

1.

2.

3.

4.

5.

Try creating a schedule to do these fun things at least once a week. I would prefer you do something fun once a day, but we'll start slow. Maybe you can pick one thing from your list and do one a week for the next 5 weeks. You should pick a time and date that you will do this one fun thing because if you procrastinate on it, you'll keep putting it off until you forget about it.

You may want to take this idea a step farther. Write 20 of your favorite ideas down on separate pieces of paper, put them in a jar, so each morning you must pull one out and do that fun thing. It's a great visual reminder to stay light hearted and have fun at work. This is actually a great team building exercise as well. It's a win-win for everyone. One month of building better friendships.

How to Make Meetings More Fun

Most meetings suck. They drain you of energy and most of the time nothing gets accomplished. After doing some research on the topic, I see that a lot of people agree with me.

The Speed Thinking Zone describes why they think most meetings don't work: (1)

- The meetings are too long.
- One person can dominate.
- Meetings don't start on time.
- Individual contribution is often not encouraged or valued.
- Some managers are too aggressive with the person rather than the issue.
- The wrong people are at the meeting.
- People were not prepared.
- The purpose of the meeting was not clear.

Statistics from EffectiveMeetings.com explains why meetings are so ineffective: (2)

- Most professionals who meet on a regular basis admit to daydreaming (91%).
- People miss meetings (96%) or miss parts of meetings (95%).
- A large percentage of respondents (73%) say they have brought other work to meetings.
- 39% say they have dozed during meetings.

All of these problems come back to a core problem: Meetings aren't fun. If people aren't having fun, they end up disliking what they do.

Most of the websites I have researched talk about making the meetings more organized. They are missing the point. You can make meetings shorter and more organized, but if people still hate going then they will still daydream and miss meetings.

When people are having fun, they are more creative and communicate better. They want to help each other to find a solution.

I've put together 7 ideas that will help your meetings become more enjoyable and more effective.

First we must figure out what we want our meetings to be:

- Productive – you are getting stuff done.
- Enjoyable – you want to look forward to the next meeting not dread it.
- Creative – you are thinking outside of the norm to find solutions that will solve difficult problems.

To bring these three elements to every one of your meetings, you need to set some guidelines. Here is a sheet you can bring to your next meeting. Have everyone fill it out then discuss what needs to be included in each category.

1. Set Guidelines
2. Let everyone know the purpose of the meeting 24 hours in advance
3. Have Goals
4. Use the "Yes, and…" Technique
5. Take Standing Breaks
6. Review the Positive – what went well and what is most vital
7. Keep Improving – ask people to suggest one improvement

Every organization is different, so I tried to include the most powerful elements to make your meetings kick butt.

Set Guidelines

Every meeting needs standards, otherwise people get off track. If your company can implement 30 minute meetings then go for it. You'll notice that when you are restricted to a short time period, you will get more accomplished in a shorter time.

I like to take my meetings one step further and take the last five minutes to review and make decisions. Too many meetings are used as an excuse to delay starting or finishing projects.

You know what your organization needs to accomplish. You have to find a way to make it happen as quickly as possible.

Let everyone know the purpose of the meeting 24 hours in advance

90% of the meetings I've been to have been thrown together without preparation. No agenda, No explanation, No goals.

People love a loose structure that allows them to be creative, but not at the expense of getting stuff done.

Have Goals

Of the remaining 10%, 5% are actually effective and the other 5% have been planned but don't have any goals. If at the end of each meeting you are in the same place that you started, yes, you are spinning your wheels.

You need to have a specific goal in mind before you start. Try to limit your goals to just one or two. Too many goals will cause confusion and only make people more upset. When you set limits on your goals, you know what you need to accomplish and it's attainable.

How can this make meetings more fun?

Good question.

It's more fun because you are actually accomplishing work. There is hardly a better feeling than a finished project that is being used by a customer/client/co-worker.

Use the "Yes, and…" Technique

The basic principle of the "Yes, and…" technique is to let the creative juices flow and flow and flow. That means you can't put down anyone's ideas. You have to accept their idea and add on top of it.

This strategy forces people to think in an abundant mindset instead of allowing people to rip each other's ideas apart.

Meetings become less dreadful and more encouraging. People aren't worried about looking bad in front of others because they know that their idea won't be laughed at; it will be built upon.

Take Standing Breaks

By the end of most meetings, everyone is slumped in their chairs looking forward to when they can leave. The best way to offset these feelings is to keep people moving. Have everyone stand for five minutes as you continue to discuss topics. Notice how people will think differently. They will be more engaged.

When everyone is ready to sit back down, take a minute to do a few stretches. You'll get your blood flowing and the energy will pick up another level.

Review the Positive

At the end of each meeting there is usually a, "Thank God, I can go back and do real work" attitude after the meeting is done. This can be eliminated by asking everyone to share one positive thing that they took from the meeting. Make sure you let everyone know about this in advance because they will make sure to pay attention throughout the meeting.

The best part is that each person has such a different perspective. I'm often caught off guard by the take-away from most of my co-workers.

Keep Improving

Ask your people how the meetings can be improved. Do this after every meeting for the first month, and then make sure to do it after the first meeting of each month. People know what they want to accomplish and how to do it best. When you can empower people to improve the process, your meetings will become more productive.

The hard part is actually implementing these ideas. Make sure you vote on these ideas at the next meeting and write them in the "meeting guidelines." I would suggest sending out these meeting bylaws at the beginning of each month. People will forget unless you have someone keeping track of these ideas.

Making it Happen

Habits are hard to break and your organization is probably used to the way meetings are run. Don't use this as an excuse. Make it your mission to make your meetings fun. The more fun they are, the more your people will want to join in and come up with ideas that can take your company to the next level.

Just because the material is dry doesn't mean your interactions with each other need to be boring too.

Allow jokes to fly and don't be too worried about controlling the meetings. Enforcing too many rules will make people hate the process again.

What can you subtract from your meetings so they are more fun and productive? (e.g. Reviews of people's project status. Only talk about concepts that need attention.)

Once you subtract the weaknesses from your meeting, you can make room to add more enjoyable practices.

What can you add to your meetings to make them more fun and productive? (I have a friend who loves to do push-ups, squats, and other exercises with his team.)

You want people to want to go to meetings. It's a way to connect, build friendships, and improve ideas. Just make them interesting and useful so people don't avoid them like the plague.

(1) http://www.thespeedthinkingzone.com/faster-meetings/why-dont-meetings-work/
(2) http://effectivemeetings.com/meetingbasics/meetstate.asp

Dealing with Stress

- 75% of people who go to the hospital are there for stress-related symptoms. (American Medical Association)
- 62% of Americans say that work has a significant impact on stress levels. (APA Survey 2004)

Your ability to process your stress will dictate a large portion of your happiness and success in your career. If you can process it quickly, you will probably stay healthier. Because there is less stress on your body and your mind, you will be able to make choices that stay true to your core self.

I was asked to write about a certain company on my website for a good fee at the time, but I turned them down. I really needed the money, but I refused because it wasn't a good fit.

When I started my website, I told myself that I would always stay true to my values. I felt a twinge of pressure to accept this offer because it was quite a bit of money, but I took a few minutes to relax with the idea and I knew that the long-term health of my business was more important. I was happy to say "no" when even down deep I knew that my family needed the money.

I understood what was most important to me and stuck to it.

You must discover what is really important and what can be dismissed.

What worry can you let go of right now? (e.g. money issues, co-worker difficulties, productivity problems)

If you focus on your worries, you are going to increase stress. It's a simple equation: What you focus on = Your happiness or lack there of. You must create a mindset that is abundant and you'll lower your stress and increase your happiness.

How can you remind yourself to keep letting go of this worry until it sticks? (e.g. every time you think of a certain worry drop 25 cents into a jar. Watch how fast the money piles up.).

What strategies can you come up with to release your stress on a daily basis?

Process Your Stress Faster

A few years ago, I remember like it was yesterday because I freaked out, I was having an amazing day until my boss asked me to have the report I was currently working on done by the end of the day. I wasn't even close to being finished. My stress level shot up and I began to work like a wild turkey – no rhythm or reason to my actions. The funny thing was that I was probably going to finish before the end of the day anyway. Earlier that morning, I predicted that I would be done around 3pm. The extra stress only freaked me out and it didn't help me work any faster.

I finished the report at 3:30, and I attribute the extra half hour to me getting all worked up and having to calm myself down. That's what spurred on the idea for this segment. I wanted to share both the mistakes and the positive aspects of how I processed my stress. I lost a half hour and I don't want the same to happen to you. If you lose an hour every day because of stress, that adds up to 365 hours every year. That's over nine work that could have been more productive if you could have released your stress faster. I'm not even factoring in the toll that is taken on the mind and body or the level of happiness that is probably decreased because of your worry.

It's up to you to notice the stress and work with its effects. You can do this by applying a few simple techniques.

Become a Student of Your Reactions

When my boss told me that the report was due by the end of the day, my heartbeat picked up and a rush of thoughts bombarded me. My first instinct was to go to the bathroom and calm down. My thoughts were rebelling: "Who is he to tell me when to get my work done? Uh, duh – my boss!", "Maybe I can't get it done.", "I need more time." After I calmed down, I came out of the bathroom and I knew that I needed a plan.

Plan out what needs to get done: (I wrote out a list of what I needed to do to make it happen.)
1. Just keep doing what I was doing (it was just a reminder that I knew that just thirty minutes ago I wasn't worried, but now I am freaking out).
2. Finish writing the report.
3. Double check figures.
4. Print it out.
5. Check for grammatical errors.
6. Submit to the boss.

I was able to see the whole picture, which helped me calm down and get my focus back on task.

Look for the Positive Side

My boss wanted me to get this report done and I knew that, unless some emergency popped up, it would in his inbox by the end of the day. I also knew that this opportunity would help me look good.

Instead of focusing on what could go wrong, I focused on the positives of what could go right.

Process on the Way to Your Favorite Stress Relief

Many people go on their walk or to their Yoga class with their stress engines running full steam. When they get halfway into their stress-relief routine, they finally start to slow down. If you can start the process of relaxing yourself on the way to stress relief, you'll be more willing to release at the beginning of your relaxation routine. You'll have deeper and longer-lasting relief. As you're putting on shoes or grabbing your Yoga mat, create relaxed feelings by focusing on the moment or imagining how you will feel when you are on your walk or in your Yoga class.

Your Patterns

We all fall into habits of allowing stress to get the best of us. It usually happens to many of us while we're in the car. When you notice these recurring patterns, you must begin to work with them. Getting upset because someone doesn't drive fast enough is a waste of energy. If you can't pass them, then you must take a different approach. You can do this by reminding yourself that they're trying to live life the best way they know how. Most likely they aren't trying to upset you. Then send them a little thought of thanks for reminding you to harness your stress instead of letting it get the best of you.

Vent to a Friend

Sometimes stress becomes so overwhelming that we need to vent. I vent by writing and talking to my co-workers. After my boss gave me the challenge to have the report done by the end of the day, I peeked over my cubicle wall later that afternoon and complained to my co-worker. She agreed with me, like all good confidants do, and after five minutes I felt better and I got to work on the report.

Daily Practice

You process stress differently than anyone else, so try a few of these techniques to help you reach past your current level of stress relief. The more you work with your stress relief, the better you'll become at releasing your frustrations.

By giving yourself as many options as possible to process your stress, you'll be able to soften the pain that comes along with stress.

What patterns do you notice that happen again and again during stressful moments? (e.g. your boss creates a lot of stress, deadlines are always fast approaching)

By understanding your patterns you can then create systems that allow you to release stress quickly.

What are your three favorite stress relievers? (e.g. walking outside, venting to a friend, making a list of things that you appreciate in the present moment)

How can you catch the stress rising before it overwhelms you? (e.g. you notice your shoulders getting tight, you get hot flashes, you put the blame on others)

We all have our stress signals that we must by hyper aware of. The quicker you notice the stress taking hold, the easier time you will have releasing it before your stress becomes too strong.

25 Weird Breaks for Stress Relief

When you keep trying to apply the same solutions to old problems all you get is the same results. If you want to develop your emotional strength, you have to be a scientist. Experiment with many different solutions and notice what works and what doesn't. If the old solutions don't work, it's time to try something new.

I wrote a guest post for the 100,000 subscriber Zen Habits (at the time, not it's over 200,000 as of this printing, *6 Amazing Techniques to Staying Happy During a Stressful Project*. The feedback was tremendous.

Out of all the techniques, the one that got the best response was "Take a Weird Break." I wasn't expecting that.

Here is what I wrote:

Take a "Weird" Break

I often get mentally locked up because I can't focus on what is right before me. There are too many options. If I have to write an email, generate a report, and work on a marketing plan, then I feel hot and cloudy. My overwhelmed mind just wants to shut down. I usually get up and take a "weird" break to clear my head.

During my break, I do something a little weird like take a short walk and hang from a tree branch. I find that it's tough to worry while hanging from a beautiful tree. Plus, my creativity almost always starts flowing again.

There are so many ways we can pull ourselves out of a stressful state if we just take a moment to be creative.

We have to find creative solutions to our ever evolving stress. I put together a list of 25 weird breaks we can use to improve our work happiness.

25 Weird Break Ideas

1. Stand on one leg where people can see you and just breathe.

This is also an exercise in not caring about what others think. Hopefully this will make you even more focused to stay in the present moment.

2. Call a friend who you haven't talked to in over a year (This feels weird because it's usually awkward for the first few minutes).

Sometimes we need to reconnect with an old friend to help us see life from a new perspective.

3. Laugh really hard at a joke that is only mildly funny.

Don't do this to be a jerk. I'm suggesting you laugh really hard at a mildly funny joke because sometimes we don't put enough effort into laughing. It can spur on some much needed stress relief if we just tip the endorphin scales in our favor.

4. Drink water upside down.

Taking a sip of water while upside down will reduce hiccups and stress.

5. Go outside and just feel the grass for 60 seconds.

Allow yourself to feel like a kid again. Little kids are fascinated by everything they touch. They don't have time to let worried thoughts stress them out.

When you go outside and just enjoy the natural beauty of the grass, you won't be able to think about your career, family or anything else: Just you and the earth.

6. Putt a golf ball from the opposite side.

Try to do anything from the opposite side. You have to focus very hard. Even writing your name with the other hand takes you out of your stressed out state.

7. Climb a tree barefoot.

This can hurt if you don't pick the right tree. So find a tree with smooth bark and enjoy.

8. Make as many cool sounds with a piece of paper as you can.

The ideas are endless. My favorite is making it sound like a storm. Just hold a piece of paper at the top and shake from side to side.

9. Hug a tree.

We all should be tree huggers at some point in our lives.

10. Buy two of the craziest drinks on the way into work and share one with your co-worker on your first break.

Living in Texas gives me access to a strong Mexican culture, so I picked up two bottles of some weird Mango drink for a co-worker and me. It was delicious.

11. Meditate in your car or in the grass and focus on what it would feel like to fly like a bird.

Using your imagination to take a break is the easiest weird break anyone can do. You can fly like a bird, become invisible or create a new planet. They will all help reduce your stress.

12. Admit a weird thing you did as a kid to a co-worker.

I did a lot of weird stuff as a kid. I used to jump from high places and land on stones to see how tough I was. :)

13. Make a snowman out of tissue paper and tape.

A weird piece of art can take us out of our normal thought process and help us relax.

14. Walk around the office backwards.
I just did this one yesterday. (I did this one at home). I don't think I'm cool enough to pull this one off at the office.

15. Pluck one leaf from a tree for every friend you work with.

This is just plain weird and I would probably be afraid to do this, but you may have some pretty weird co-workers who might enjoy this.

16. Ask a co-worker if they could talk to someone about their stress, living or dead, who it would be.

I would choose Abraham Lincoln. He went through severe depression and came out a stronger person.

17. Play a joke on a co-worker – cover everything in Saran Wrap.

Most of us need to laugh a little more at our jobs, and a good practical joke on a friend can bring on the laughter we need.

18. Switch everything on your desk from one side to the other (just for one day).

Life is all about perception. It's always good to get a change of perspective when you feel stressed.

19. Find a weird object on a walk break and keep it on your desk.

I found a really white snail shell. It's quite beautiful. Every time I see it, I feel calm. It reminds me that there are more important things in life than taking my stress too seriously.

20. List all the craziest things you've done in your life on a piece of paper, and then burn it.

I've never done this one, but I really want to try it. I'm going to do this one this weekend. (Note: Always practice fire safety. I don't recommend you starting any fires in the office unless you expect to be laid off in the next few days.) ;)
21. Email a co-worker a link to an odd story you found on the internet.

There are some weird people out there. I found one story about a meth addict who had a drug lab in his house. He called the cops because a friend stole his wallet from his house. The cops entered the house and arrested the dummy.

22. Create a paper crown for a co-worker who has the blues.

I've never tried this one either, but I know a co-worker who could use this one right now.

23. Photocopy your hand.

A classic that never goes out of style.

24. Draw a cartoon of your boss (But don't show it to him/her).

I did this one at home. It helped put my stress into perspective. Sometimes I take people too seriously.

25. Spin in your chair until your momentum brings you to a stop.

This is also a classic. I like this one because it makes me a little queasy, but I never regret doing it.

Your Weird Breaks

Weird breaks are a wonderful way to take yourself out of your normal routine and help you find a healthier and happier perspective. Think of it as a mini-vacation for the brain.

You may think some of these are too weird for you, and that's fine. Only do what feels comfortable.

We are all weird in our own way. Some of us are better at hiding it. I say let the weirdness out, so you can just be yourself.

Which "weird break" would push you just slightly outside of your comfort zone?

By taking a "weird break" you break the worrying cycle because you can't help but be in the present moment and laugh at yourself.

What kind of "weird break" can you come up with on your own to help relieve your stress?

Stress Management Journal

Everyone stresses out about something every now and again, but do you stress out about the same things over and over? If you do it's probably a pattern that's hard to break. One of my most productive tools was a stress journal. I documented everything that kept stressing me out. If my mom called complaining about her health, I would write it down. If my boss piled a bunch of work on me, I would write it down. I skewed a lot of my memories to fit my needs. I wrote everything down so I wouldn't forget. I wanted to remember how I felt in every stressful situation, down to all the tiny little details. This required me to be as honest as possible so I could learn to improve my emotional state.

As the months passed I began to see patterns in my stress. I became stressed out when I was driving (especially during my commute to and from work), when I felt work was unfair, when I was late to a meeting or a doctor's appointment, during a tense sporting event, while watching a high energy movie, and at social parties such as Christmas work gatherings.

Instead of resigning myself to feeling stressed out in these situations, I began working with my relaxation skills. Whenever a technique was successful, I documented how it worked and how it helped me release my stress and stay relaxed. When my jaw tightened during a stressful project, I reminded myself to relax and then I massaged my jaw for ten seconds. I did this over and over again until it started setting in. Eventually I stopped tightening my jaw and began to feel relaxed during even the most stressful moments. When I got saddled with extra work, my brow would normally furrow. When I recognized this reaction I focused on taking deep breaths in and out to calm myself down. I made a plan to help organize my situation get everything done or I talked to my boss about needing help. I learned to cut the stress off before it piled up too strong and overwhelmed me.

Using a stress journal can help you obtain a better understanding of what stresses you out, but it doesn't keep the stress away. You must do that by working with your emotions. Take the time to notice what causes your stress, and then apply the stress relieving techniques that work best for you.

If you think that keeping a journal will take too much time, then try writing just one sentence a day. Focus on the good things you've been able to accomplish.

Start right now. Write three sentences about the stress. How you've had to deal with it and how you presently deal with it, then how you plan to deal with it next time a similar situation pops up.

1.

2.

3.

Leisure is a Must

We all need to slow down throughout the day and take some time to relax. That's what scheduling in leisure time is all about. We need to make sure that our bosses understand that we aren't robots and we need some time to joke around, some coffee break time, and just plain fun time. I was able to procure an interview with Allison Link. I thought that she would be very helpful to my Work Happy Now readers and lo and behold I was right.

I only wanted her to answer one question in order to help you understand the benefits of leisure time at work, and she answered it better than I could have expected. I asked her, "How does someone schedule in leisure time when they don't have enough time to get everything done that their boss asks of them?"

Allison's answer:

Become more aware of the benefits of leisure. If you have a strong value for leisure, others will see you as a role model when they understand that your quality of life is higher than theirs. You will help them believe it is possible to have leisure in your life and not be less productive (short term and long term). You should make time for leisure because it provides the balance we need to handle non-leisure activities well and enhances resilience and life satisfaction.

While there are a few happy workaholics, most people need time away from work in order to meet all of their needs. They may have talents that do not get expressed on the job, partners or families they want to spend time with, projects to complete and values they want to support. They also need to unwind, relax, refresh and revitalize themselves.

A leisure-positive lifestyle:

- Increases physical and psychological well-being. It reduces stress and increases wellness, and enhances people's sense of independence.
- Has been shown to help people resist stress-induced illness.
- Impacts professional performance, enhancing decision-making and problem-solving capabilities.
- Supports personal development by clarifying values, increasing social interaction and breaking down barriers

When people live a balanced life, they provide an important benefit to their communities as well, simply by demonstrating that such a life is possible and valuable.

My follow-up:

My readers are constantly bombarded with the need to get more done in less time. I was hoping that you might have some insight.

Allison's answer:

There is evidence to show that leisure is linked to productivity. Adults have been shown to be able to maintain higher attention levels when they have more frequent breaks. Several U.S. and Canadian studies show that leisure programs "increased productivity by seven percent while decreasing absenteeism by 20 percent."

Leisure education as provided by The Leisure Link builds employee morale and strengthens team functioning through its positive impacts on:

- Self concept, self esteem and self confidence
- Sense of autonomy and perception of freedom
- Stress reduction and relief of boredom

Employees may find a renewed sense of purpose for its own sake. Also, increasing leisure can increase creativity.

Everyone can use more creativity in their lives (even at work, even if you have trouble getting everything done that your boss asks of you). Whatever you do, being able to generate a lot of ideas about it will help you do it better.

The mind needs to unwind and just have fun. There is a reason why kids are given time to eat and then run around the playground. They need to release their stress and so do you. You need to schedule in some leisure time every single day.

Here are 7 of my favorite leisure breaks:

- Take a long lunch break and go to a museum by yourself.
- Stretch at your desk for two minutes.
- Meet with a friend who you normally don't see for lunch.
- Breathe deeply for two minutes and do nothing else in that time.
- Walk around the block.
- Call your mother or another relative (only if s/he doesn't stress you out).
- Read a funny book during your break.
- Write a poem.

It's up to you to schedule in a little leisure time for yourself, so you will work happier and be more productive. Believe me, your family will thank you for de-stressing throughout the day instead of letting it all come out when you get home.

Leisure will help you create the conditions for nurturing creativity in your life and in your work. People are at their most creative when they are in a "flow state."

Your work and leisure both have a ripple effect into each other. Think about what kind of ripple you want that to be.

Taking time to just chill and do something that takes your thoughts in a new direction really helps you enhance your creativity and let go of your stress.

What kind of leisure break can you take each day?

When is the best time to take this break? (Plan it and make it happen)

Exercise While You Are At Work

Your blood needs to flow freely and, at times, quickly. Fast-moving blood will help clean out the plaque that's been building up inside your arteries. Sometimes our jobs just don't provide the excitement that gets the blood flowing. So we need to create it for ourselves.

I don't want you to strip down to your underwear and streak through the office. Well I think that would be cool, but it wouldn't be very good for your career.

Exercise is a vital component to feeling good while we are working throughout the day. People who exercise at least 20 minutes a day see a significant increase in energy compared to people who don't exercise at all.

> *"Exercise can relax you. One exercise session generates 90 to 120 minutes of relaxation response. Some people call this post-exercise euphoria or endorphin response. We now know that many neurotransmitters, not just endorphins, are involved. The important thing though is not what they're called, but what they do: They improve your mood and leave you relaxed."*
> - American Council On Fitness (1)

I want you to incorporate small segments of exercise while you are at work. *What? I can't exercise at work.* Yes you can. There are plenty of ways to take a few minutes to get a little exercise in.

Squats in the Bathroom

Exercise in the bathroom? Gross. It may be, but it's my favorite in-office exercise. The bathrooms at my work are single person bathrooms and I can lock the door behind me. Squats can be done in an office or anywhere else, but just find a place where you won't be disturbed.

Results: I do squats for one minute and my heart is pounding. The thighs are the largest muscle in your body and when you work them out you are getting the most bang for your time.

Go for a Walk

Take a walk around your office. This is the most obvious and popular way to exercise at work. I always like to take a quick fifteen minute walk around the block. I try to do this at a fast pace to get my heart pumping. If I do this in the summer I make sure to keep a stick of deodorant in my desk so I don't stink.

Results: Going for a walk is my favorite stress reliever. It helps me clear out the worry and brings me back into a happier state.

Stretching in Your Chair

Carpal tunnel and other ailments develop as a result of repetitive movements. Taking a few minutes to stretch your wrists, back and shoulders will break up your day and keep your joints healthier.

Results: I've abused my right wrist because of my overuse of the mouse. I try to stretch for a few minutes every hour. This habit has helped me gain a fresh perspective on my work as well as keep my wrists healthy.

One-Minute Relaxation

Just like your muscles and joints need exercise, so does your brain. You should be taking the time to process your activity throughout the day. Exercising does this, but an active relaxation will help you clear out your mind to help you transition to that next task. Productivity is a key component to happiness at work, and when we combat stress throughout the day we get more done and are much happier.

Results: I used to just race through the day, making myself frantic and by the end of the day I was ready for a beer. I relied on that beer to calm me down. Because of my one-minute relaxations throughout the day, I'm more relaxed when I get home and I no longer need a beer to transition to home life.

Push-ups

I love push-ups. They are probably my favorite muscle-strengthening exercise. I try to do these on my lunch break. I'm no longer a bashful person so I'll do them on the sidewalk or in a field.

Results: Strength-based exercises are vital to strong bones – our support system. We make our lives easier when we have a strong foundation. I've noticed that my confidence increases after push-ups. Just five push-ups make a big difference. I feel like I can tackle any problem.

What exercise can you do at work?

How can you work this exercise into your work day so you can do it during a break, lunch hour or during your work day?

(1) Exercise Can Help Control Stress
http://www.acefitness.org/FITFACTS/fitfacts_display.aspx?itemid=51

Dealing with Your Commute

In order to get the results you desire, you need to find a way to set your mood to an optimal happiness level before you get into work. If you are angry before you even get to work, you are setting the tone for the whole day.

I recently read a bumper sticker on the back of a rusted old pick-up truck. It said:

"I've got nowhere special to be, so why don't you get off my butt!"

I was actually riding his bumper because I was rushing to get to work. I had already hit three red lights and now I was staring at that rusty old truck. Since I couldn't pass him, I eased off my gas and thought about that bumper sticker. The more I read it, the more it made sense. That man understood that whenever he got to his destination, regardless of the time, it was going to be just fine. There is no need to put pressure on myself to get there faster when the laws of physics and a big old rusty truck won't allow it.

Creating Stress

When you get mad at someone for driving too slowly, you're creating stress that you can't control.
Why punch at the sand when you can create a sandcastle?

You do need some tension to function, but too much will harm you. So don't overtax your body's resources. If you can learn to balance your stress you'll improve your mood.

Finding Those Gems

I believe that many of us feel the same stress when we commute to work. If you can't relax behind the wheel then you need to learn some stress relief techniques to use when you're commuting. For example, I keep a tennis ball in my car and I'll squeeze it to occupy my muscles and relieve my tension. You may want to put on your favorite CD and try to zone out to the beautiful sounds instead of allowing your anger to bubble over.

Everyone should learn a few stress relief techniques and apply them when they are commuting to work. The key to developing emotional intelligence is applying the right techniques at the right time.

Castle Building

My absolute favorite technique is to find things that I appreciate as I am driving to work. Maybe it's an Oak tree that I always pass but never noticed, or an old home with brown paint peeling off of it. Whatever it is, I make sure I give a little thanks for it being there.

This technique is what I call "castle building" – making something beautiful out of something frustrating. You can learn to curb your stress when you get stuck behind a truck by appreciating the things that you would normally speed on by. You can also use this "castle building" technique on the train, bus or bike. Whatever your mode of transportation, try this technique on your next commute and let me know how it helps.

What techniques can you use to curb your commuter anger?

How do you think this will help you stay calm?

There is Creativity in Every Job

There is something beautiful about creating something that wasn't there before.

There is creativity in every job. The person who finds a way to be creative at his/her job will find a way to improve their results. A creative bus driver will be tuned in to the flow of traffic. A creative car mechanic will find a solution that the average mechanic just didn't take the time to see.

Unleashing your creativity is vital to working happy because you are solving problems instead of just getting by. You need to find that creative connection that allows you to engage your heart and mind.

Expanding Your Creativity Through Active Relaxation

If you are enjoying this book, you would probably enjoy one or more of the following: a meditative walk in the woods, a long hot shower, Yoga, sitting meditation, Tai Chi, or some form of exercise that engages your mind and body. You also understand the importance of being relaxed when trying to be creative. If you push too hard to accomplish a project, you usually end up with poor results. You don't have time to think through your options.

Many of you may be thinking, "I do my best work when I'm under a little pressure." This may be true on occasion, but can you imagine what it would be like if you had to work under pressure all the time? Do you really think you would always put your best work out there? If you told a painter or novelist to rush their work, do you think the final product would turn out better? No, because they weren't relaxed while creating.

My favorite Active Relaxing activity is a walk with my dog. My mind is focused on enjoying my surroundings and not on some project that I need to complete.

I come up with the best ideas for articles when I'm taking the time to look around at my surroundings. I'm focused on the trees, my dog, leg muscles, and breath. This allows my mind to feel free and have fun. I'm not focused on coming up with a great idea, so my thoughts can gather the inspiration from wherever it comes from.

When you need to be creative, you should have an outlet that allows you to actively relax.

List five ways that you can actively relax so you can let your thoughts find the inspiration you need. (e.g. Imagine your perfect career. What is the first step toward realizing this career?)

Creativity Triggers

The creativity triggers to get yourself into a creative mood aren't easy to develop. Sometimes we try so hard and we can't trigger creativity. We sit in front of our computer and the words don't come out, or you try to draw and it's all crap.

This has happened to me many, many times. I realized that I was forcing the creativity to come out. As you know creativity doesn't work this way.

You may also try to jump right into work without using a set-up to trigger your creativity.

This is a simple technique that many people don't use because they don't take the time to listen to their emotions. I think that since you've gotten this far you aren't this type of person. All you need is the outline to use creativity triggers and you'll be developing new work on a regular basis in no time.

The idea is simple. You must set your creativity when you wake up to give yourself the best chance of creating amazing work.

Emotions are a tricky beast. I know you know this. There are some days that just feel great and we can create amazing things. You just have to learn how to trigger this feeling, so you have a bit of say in when your muse will strike.

I use underwear to plan my creativity seed. I literally put on my red underwear when I want to accomplish a lot of writing. This doesn't always work. Like I said, there is no such thing as forcing creativity. But it does give me a good chance to allow the muse to flow through me.

What is your creativity anchor? (e.g. a lucky coin in your pocket, a creativity shirt, red underwear)

What is your next project can you use this anchor on?

Give it a try for a few weeks and watch your creativity flow more easily.

Imagination Can Be Your Best Friend

Most of my earlier working life had been a struggle. I swung between complicated and simple perspectives, hardly ever straddling the middle. I was afraid to let go of my limited view because I thought that if I just simplified my work, I would be happy. A simple life is good, but there will always be sadness, happiness, fear, and passion in every job.

> *"Life's like a movie, write your own ending. Keep believing, keep pretending."*
> - Jim Henson

The tool of imagination is one that we usually reserve for kids, but as adults we need to cultivate this skill because it's so versatile. It helps us see life from a perspective that can make our lives enjoyable, peaceful, and interesting.

We like to keep our lives simple and pleasant. The problem with simple and pleasant is that our brains seek passion and excitement. That's why people love to complete big projects. The stimulation brings the feeling of great accomplishment.

When I'm at work and I'm having a rough day, I imagine what I must look like from my Grandmother's perspective. I see this glow of love around me and this glow starts to penetrate into my heart, filling me with joy. This perspective usually picks me up and helps me see past my negative self-view.

When I was fired from a job in my mid-twenties, I felt like crying in the manager's office (I know I'm a big baby). I actually hugged him goodbye (He was a good man; it was the owner who didn't like me) and promptly went into a depression.

I felt disconnected for almost two months. I went on unemployment and rode around on my bicycle every day. It wasn't until I hit my lowest point that my creativity finally kicked in. Love showed up in everything and everyone. The grocery store checkout lady smiled at me. My parents helped me pay my rent. I felt like I was surrounded by love. I decided to write a book about how I found my joy. I turned my life into a story. That book spurred this blog and the rest of my passion.

Your imagination is a tool that can help open doors to new parts of your life. Doors that will help you tap into the work passion that you need, or just turn a bad day into an exciting learning experience. The best way to do this is to start off slowly because if you start too fast you might give up. I want you to slowly tap your mind for imaginative solutions to old problems.

What do you struggle with on a daily basis? Who bothers you in your life? Try using your imagination to see a new angle. If that co-worker keeps hassling you, try to imagine that he had a rough childhood. Do you do monotonous work every day? Try imagining that you are a movie star playing the role of a lifetime. You'll be amazed at how your imagination can improve almost any situation. You'll bring a hop back in your step.

If bad situations keep popping up, then your creativity will only take you so far. You may need to change your situation by finding a new job or finding a new position within the company. But sometimes we just need to get lost in our imaginations to make the day a little more enjoyable. In my eyes, there is nothing wrong with that.

What part of your job could you inject more creativity into?

What are 3 ways you can inject more creativity into your job?

How can you implement the best creativity idea into your work?

Live Your Passions

You deserve the right to do work that gets you excited about waking up every morning. It's this work that's going to help you achieve great results.

You've probably worked at a job you've hated. The results that you produced probably stunk.

You've probably worked at a job that you've loved. The results that you produced were probably amazing.

The reason is simple. You found meaning in your work.

That leaves you with three options.

1. Finding meaning in your present job
2. Finding a job that gives you meaning. (i.e., Is a better fit with your purpose and passions?)
3. Building a business that gives you meaning.

Ok, there is a fourth option, winning the lottery, but for some reason I don't think you'll depend on this option.

No option is perfect. There are pain points that come along with each choice. You have to understand what your needs are and how to best meet them. And that's no problem for you because you've made it this far in the book, you have these tools.

In the next few chapters we'll discuss how to dissect these options and pick the one that fits you the best.

Finding the Passion to Change the Course of the World

The lofty concept of changing the world is not a new one. Most of you want to make an impact on the world in a positive way. This is great, but most of you don't know what kind of impact you can make. I'm here to tell you that you are already doing it.

You just need to optimize this impact.

You are already making the world a better place when you buy lunch for a friend, make your child giggle, and teach someone an idea that is new to them. You can expand this to help more and more people. It's what Oprah, Mother Teresa, and your parents have done. They have all taught people how to enjoy their lives.

The Bach Effect

Johann Sebastian Bach (31 March 1685 [21 March] – 28 July 1750), a German composer, wrote music each week for Sunday mass. He could have viewed this job as inferior to his skills, only creating music for 80 to 100 people. Today most accomplished musicians wouldn't create a new piece almost every week. They play the same 20 songs that the crowd always hears on the radio. Bach saw the higher purpose behind his work.

Bach created music to bring people closer to God. He wanted people to feel like they were walking hand in hand with God every Sunday. This higher purpose encouraged him to compose some of the most beautiful music ever created (in my opinion).

He made good money, but not by today's standards. There were no enforced copyrights or ability to mass distribute his music. He didn't care. He only wanted to create music to please his listeners.

Now his music is making millions of people happy. Imagine how many more people might have hated their life or wouldn't have been inspired to create music to make other people happy if it weren't for Bach's contribution.

He changed the course of the world by connecting to his higher purpose. He connected to a passion that helped people feel the beauty in their lives. What could be a greater gift to the world than that?

You have this same opportunity through working and interacting with your friends in your life.

Your Symphony

You have an even more difficult challenge. You may only have an audience of a few people to influence – your boss, a child, or a friend. It's hard to feel motivated when your audience might not appreciate your hard work.

I've worked for bosses who didn't see my value. It was hard for me to feel positive about the work that I accomplished. I failed to see the higher purpose of my work.

I've stuffed over 100,000 marketing bags in my life. Each bag was only a drop in the ocean of marketing bags. One bag might not have sold any product; another one may have made a person happy because they found a pen that they loved in the bag, while the third bag might have changed the direction of a person's life. That person might have bought a product from us that gave him hours of happiness because of my marketing bag.

I worked for a high pressure valve company that ground away at my soul. I worked in the marketing department stuffing thousands of these bags. Each minute felt like someone was sandpapering my knuckles.

At the time, I couldn't see the possibilities that might occur from my work. I never thought of the 100,000 bag symphony that I was creating.

I also answered phones for this company. One client called in and commented on the valve that he bought that saved him and his company so much pain. All the other valves broke after a few weeks. Our valve was 5 times more expensive, but lasted 20 times longer. He also commented that he attended the conference where we exhibited, and he felt so lucky to have found us.

My hard work was worth all the effort.

Was this work my life calling? No, but I saw the value in what I was doing.

Your Challenge

You have to find the "why" behind the work that you are doing, no matter what it is. That means tracing back the possible outcomes and seeing what pings the part of your soul that makes you happy.

Next time you are doing a job you feel is tedious, boring, or exhausting, list as many ways that you can think of in which your job might help someone else. Keep listing until one of those reasons brings a little motivation to your work.

1.

2.

3.

4.

5.

6.

7.

8.

9.

10.

11.

12.

13.

14.

15.

16.

17.

18.

19.

20.

Find a Deeper Meaning in Your Work

You have to believe that there is a deeper purpose to your work. The paycheck alone will not keep you motivated. If you truly want to increase your productivity and happiness at work, you need to know what excites you.

If you believe in the work that you do, it will be easier to connect to each task. People who are passionate about their work will do almost anything to make sure the job is done well.

The problem many of us have is that we can't connect with the work we are presently doing.

Maybe you don't believe in the service or product. If this is true, you need to find a new career. You may also find the company's values have gone askew; you'll have to find a way to reconnect or take your career in a new direction.

If there is any glimmer of love for what you do then we need to expand on these feelings.

I met a BMW salesman, on a bus ride back from New York City, who took a pay cut to sell Honda cars. He didn't believe that BMW's value was worth the extra expense. He did believe in Honda's value to price ratio. So instead of selling a car he didn't believe in, he switched jobs to have an easier time connecting with his product. The best part is that within six months he was making more money because his customers sent their friends and family members to him. He received twice as many word of mouth sales. This happened because he believed in his product.

You need to find a way to connect with your job. I would suggest that you start by listing all of the aspects of your products and services that deliver value. A few of these items should ping your heart.

If a few of these items from your list tug at your emotions, then expand on them. How can you consistently keep these feelings at the forefront of your brain as you work?

You should keep these emotional stimulators in a place where you can see them. If you are feeling down and your energy is broken, then read over these stimulators and try to put yourself in the shoes of someone who needs your product or service.

If you find that these emotional stimulators aren't doing the trick, then you need to reassess your views of your employer and consider looking for a better fit of values elsewhere.

So how do we find meaning? I'm glad you asked.

I've created five questions that will help you find more meaning in you day to day work. *I know they work because they worked for me.*

1. Make a list the people who depend on you. (Use their actual names)

Customers:

Co-workers:

Vendors:

2. Write a sentence about these 3 topics, explaining why you are good at your job.

Job related expertise:

Social skills:

One instance when you were at your best:

3. Leave a voice mail or email of appreciation for someone who has helped you at your job. (Explain what they did that helped you and why it meant so much to you.)

4. Make a list of everything you've learned while working at your job.

How your job has helped your personal development:

How your job has helped your career development:

5. Write a short paragraph that describes the best part of your job.

What does the work entail?

Why is this your favorite part of your job?

We all lose motivation, even when we love our job. It's up to each individual to find meaning in his or her work, even when it is a struggle.

There are only a few jobs that are a good fit for each individual. If you constantly struggle to find the desire to do good work then you are cheating yourself. This doesn't help either you or your company succeed. If your job - or something about the company's business practices or ethics - does not sit well with your values, it will eat away at you and cause a lot of dis-ease and then disease.

It is important that you find a job that matches with your interests, values, superpowers. Believe me, there are plenty of ways to find a new company or start your own business.

Guide Your Energy Train

We all have to do tasks that drain us of energy, but you must tip the scales to do more of the work that gets you excited. Sometimes it takes a little creativity to make your work a little more fun, or sometimes it means not doing a particular job so you can do something that makes you feel energized.

I hate analyzing data. It feels like a waste of time. In my business, I need to analyze a lot of data - both other people's data, as well as my own.

There are regular studies done on happiness (It feels like they are done on a daily basis, doesn't it?). I try to stay on top of the research so I don't get left behind. I have to analyze all this new data and compare it to what I know to make sure it's a good fit for my readers.

I also have to analyze how many people are coming to my website, what they are reading, and how I can get more people on the work happiness train.

In both cases, these tasks usually feel tedious. So instead of blocking out a large chunk of time on my schedule, I try to do it in 20 minute bursts. This way it doesn't feel so overwhelming. Some days the task feels tedious and not enjoyable, so after 20 minutes I dump it for a better task. But other days I get started and I begin to see trends and ideas begin to flow. If an idea happens, I follow my energy train. If my energy wants to go there then I don't deny myself. If, after analyzing the data, I know that my audience will love a certain type of article, I don't continue to analyze the data. I run with this energy and type like a mad man. I love that I can feel this and let myself get swept away in this new work.

You must find ways to steer your energy toward tasks that make you feel smart and powerful.

It's important to find work that allows you to transition into tasks that get you truly excited. Every job has tough parts, but if you are doing too many tough parts then you may need to find a job that allows you to switch to more stimulating work.

What work do you do now that kills your energy? Why does this work kill your energy?

How can you reduce the amount of time that you do this work?

How can you transition into energizing work more often?

If you can't transition into work that gets you excited then you must find a way to transition into a new career.

Find Work You Love

Connecting your **thoughts** to **feelings** to **actions** is a time tested problem. We no longer need to live in this struggle. We can take our careers in any direction we desire. This can actually be overwhelming.

Many of you probably have many hobbies/past-times, but not one thing that you are passionate about. This is normal.

As I was trying to find work that I loved, I was so caught up in finding the perfect career that I gridlocked my ability to choose.

A conversation that I repeated with many of my friends went like this:

Me: I love to write poetry, but I can't make money from it. How does a person make money from this?
Friend: I don't know. You can't.
Me: I don't have to make money from writing. I could write a book.
Friend: You could. What would you write about?
Me: Self-help makes a lot of money. I could write self-help.

Notice the pattern? It's all about money. This is such the wrong approach on so many levels.

The belief that I have to be practical has been ingrained in me by my parents, but from the wrong angle. I needed to go after what I loved to do and figure out how to make money from it later. Whether you are passionate about clothing, comic books, writing, teaching English, helping kids with autism, adult learning video games, or potato peelers – there is a market you can either fit into or create yourself.

Joe Ades sold potato peelers on the streets of New York. It's said he once made $100,000 in a weekend. He lived the good life – including a luxurious NY condo and indulgences like expensive Champagne and entertainment. The most fascinating part of the story is that he never retired. He loved taking his boxes of peelers to the streets and giving his spiel. And why should he retire when he loved his work.

"I can't imagine retiring," Joe said in 2008. "Retiring is like stopping living."

He applied his superpowers to a product he believed in and success came naturally. He loved the streets, learning the trade in Manchester, England. So he took his art of selling to the people. They ate it up.

He tried selling kids books, but they were too heavy. When he came across the light weight peeler, he found his niche. This discovery didn't happen until his late forties.

His amazing life didn't come without struggle. He was married to his 4th wife when he died. His way of life probably wasn't easy on his family. His life wasn't easy on him either, but he loved his work. He carried around 1,000's of vegetable peelers through rain, snow, and crowds of people.

He created the life that he wanted.

You can also create the life that you want.

Make a list of all the hobbies and jobs that you enjoy doing. This can include watching TV, writing, baking, whatever. If it involves an action that you enjoy then put it down.

1.

2.

3.

4.

5.

Circle the 3 actions that you are most passionate about. Write them here:

Now research them on Google. Write down the businesses that revolve around these topics:

What businesses fit with your superpowers?

Your Inner Compass

You probably have many passions in life. You may love your family, build a great career, write thought provoking poetry, become an amazing cook, tinker with old cars, or tell bad jokes at Thanksgiving...whatever your purpose is you must have a clear understanding of each one. They all help guide your choices.

Each passion is a guide to help you make decisions. I knew I wanted to help people, but wasn't sure what I had to offer. I had helped friends with career advice before, but never made the connection. As I looked back in my work history I realized where my greatest superpowers were listening, finding solutions and teaching. It took me a while to realize this, but once my purpose became clear it was like riding a bike downhill. Every choice became a lot easier.

Greatest purpose

You career can hold your greatest purpose because you have the chance to help a lot of people. You can teach people how to save the world, you can develop concepts to improve lives, and you can ease people's pain. Each career has many passions within it, but it's finding the one area that gets you most excited is where your purpose lies.

That means finding out why you like to do what you do.

Ask yourself, "Why am I doing my current job?"

You'll notice that you are doing it either out of fear, anger or love. Each reason on the surface feels right to you, but the more you explore "why" the more you will understand what decisions need to be made so you can do work you love.

I made the mistake of going after external rewards instead of internal ones in many phases of my career. When I first got out of college I wanted money, then I moved on to wanting adulation, then fame, then back to money, then just trying to survive. I became too afraid to take risks. When I listened to my inner compass I found that aligning my needs with others created the best results.

The only way you will do work you love is if you take risks that will emotionally hurt you. Make you feel uncomfortable. It's why fear can be such a great compass. It's how I got closer and closer to my purpose.

What are you afraid of? (Why?)

How can you use this fear to uncover your purpose? (If you are afraid of public speaking, try going to toastmasters to learn this skill. You'll notice why you were afraid which will help you uncover more of your superpowers. It's these powers that can help a lot of people live better lives.)

Build Slowly to do What You Love

This is so simple to say and write, but very hard to live. Many of us don't do what we love because of obligations, fear, and a lack of self understanding. We push through the suffering because we expect a payoff.

My parents were friends with a man who worked for a car manufacturer. He started this job at the age of nineteen, and fifteen years later he was stuck and didn't feel like he could quite. At 34, he was married with three kids when he finally realized that he had hated that last fifteen years of his working life. Severe depression tore apart his happiness.

At a picnic, we were sitting off to the side having a nice chat. Suddenly his face went sad and he confided to me that he wished that he worked with wood for a living. *That was a long time ago, but I can see how my present career was already calling to me. I wanted to learn about work happiness then too.*

This man had never worked with wood, but he had this ideal in his head. He built up this fictional person who made beautiful furniture. He fooled himself into believing that he could have lived a better life. There is nothing more painful to a person than creating what s/he thinks will make him happy and never pursuing it.

This man finally pursued woodworking after 25 years and a retirement pension. He found out that he hated working with wood. He didn't like the tedious sanding that came along with each piece.

He tortured himself for 10 years because of what he thought he would enjoy doing. That's where superpowers can bite you in the butt. If you reflect and dream without taking action, you'll never know what type of work will make you truly happy. You need reflection to aim your energy, but every solid theory must be tested.

That's why you must always use your superpowers at your present job and build from there. If you aren't using any of your superpowers at work, then use them during your leisure time. Eventually you'll start to see what you enjoy and what you are good at. You'll know what direction you need to take in order to make the most of your skills.

What can you do at your job to build toward the career you love?

If you can't do anything at your present job then what can you do at home to build toward a career in which you will use more of your superpowers and feel excited?

You will discover more about who you are and appreciate the directions in which you can take your career.

Develop a Plan to make Your Passion a Career

You are embarking on change that is going to hurt. It will be a good pain, but still none the less painful.

You will need to develop several plans to accommodate your needs.

Plans:

1. Emotional Plan
2. Relationship Plan
3. Results Plan

When you have an idea of what you will be facing and how you will handle it, your motivation to take action is easier.

Emotional Plan

What negative emotions will occur as you build the career of your dreams?

1. Frustration

What do you think will frustrate you?

How will you handle the frustration?

2. Anger

What do you think will anger you?

How will you handle these feeling of anger?

3. Sadness

What do you think will cause you to get sad?

How will you handle your sadness?

4. Negative emotion of your choosing

Think of another negative emotion that will occur.

What do you think will cause this emotion?

How will you handle this emotion?

What positive emotions will occur as you build your career?

1. Excited

What do you think will cause you to get excited?

How will you use these situations to help motivate you?

2. Confidence

What do you think will cause your confidence to build?

How will you do more of this confidence building work?

3. Positive emotion of your choosing

Think of another negative emotion that will occur.

What do you think will cause this emotion?

How will you handle this emotion?

You've been alive long enough to know that these emotions will occur. You don't want to fall back into the same mistakes you made last year or the year before.

You will be dealing with difficult co-workers, customers, vendors, and situations. You can't get around this. If you have a plan for how to handle your various scenarios you'll make better decisions.

Relationship Plan

You probably have a network already in place that will help you kick off this new career, but how far will it take you?

You need to develop friendships that will help you reach goals that seem hard to reach, but aren't impossible. These goals are attainable if you build your network now.

You need to create a plan to meet people online and in person.

What local groups can you join to meet potential allies?

What conferences can you attend?

Where else can you build your person to person network?

Where do your people hang out online?

How can you help them? (The more you can help them the more trust you will build.)

Results

Achieving the results that will "wow" is a must. You have a chance to wow people in many ways. The idea is to wow people so they remember you. When they look at you as the expert in whatever it is you love to do they will come to you when they need this thing you offer.

What is it about your peers that impresses you?

How can you implement similar ideas into your career?

What type of ideas can you come up with that scares you, but will make people notice?

There is a wall within every career. I know you will hit it. That's why passion is so important. If you can't push through this wall or climb over it or blow it up or walk around it then you aren't passionate enough about this topic or you are letting your fear get the best of you. This is tough to figure out, but a part of the process and everyone must figure this out for themselves.

You have to know when to give up and when to push through. Looking back on my career, I would have done things differently but I refused to give up. I kept adjusting and so should you. If you have passion in your heart, you must follow it. It's this love that will change people's lives.

No Need for a Summary Chapter

If you made it this far in the book, you don't need me to summarize all of the ideas that you already read. You are an intelligent person. You know what you need to do to bring your superpowers into your career.

If you work with this workbook for three months you'll be happier, more successful and you won't need me or this book any longer. After a year, you'll reach a place within you that will surprise even you. I've only planted the seed. Now it's your turn to do the hard work. Yes, it will be frustrating at times, but I promise you'll be so glad you took action on these concepts. I know they've changed my life.

You've taken responsibility for your own success and happiness. You won't need to rely on any one certain thing to be happy.

All you need is your superpowers.

Join me at:

WorkHappyNow.com

We'll develop our happiness and success together.

My Thank You to the Wonderful Teachers in my Life

Because of you I have succeeded in becoming happy with who I am. Thank you for convincing me that I have something to give the world.

- Nikki Staib – To my wife, editor, thank you for being so awesome that you've convinced me to choose you as my partner in improving the world. Even when you didn't always understand my choices you still believe in my vision.
- Gavin Staib (My son) – For helping me understand that laughing is way more important than being right.
- Erich Staib – For showing me that everyone deserves love.
- My Mom (Elsa Staib) – For teaching me that it's better to give than receive.
- My Dad (Walter Staib) – For teaching me to keep digging and believe in who I am because I am truly great.
- Linda Attwood – For all your advice and willingness to believe in my talents.
- Mike Attwood – For leading by example. Your everyday behavior is what I strive for in my life.
- Stavros Stavropoulos – For showing me that details are the most important part of every project because it separates you from the average.
- Christine (first girlfriend) – I don't need to listen to everything someone says.
- Dan Geiger – Being my website support team while I was broke. Also helping me be realistic and never stop pushing to succeed.
- Troy Kyle – Thank you for appreciating me for who I am. I cheer your name as the best manager I've ever had.
- Andy Wurst – The first CEO who cared about me more than my performance. Encouraging a young man to build his confidence.
- Hai Le – For teaching me to just jump in and see what happens.
- Seth Godin – Once you have something amazing, don't stop there. Make it so extraordinary that people can't stop talking about you.
- Tony Hsieh – Being the light that guides my way through helping people work happier.
- Chris Brogan – For being so real and kind. There is no need to be cut-throat to succeed.
- Evita Ochel – For loving everything that I write.
- My Mastermind Group – So supportive and genuine. They push me past my comfort zone.
- Kate Northrop (My college writing teacher) – Believing in me even when I didn't believe in myself.
- KJ Bartosh – Always being supportive when I needed a good friend.
- Havi Brooks – Helping me understand that self compassion is most important to happiness.
- Luke Wolfgang – Listening to my banter even when it didn't make sense.
- Lance Ekum – Showing me that connecting is the most important part of life.
- Alex Kjerulf – Helping guide me the process of making the world a happier place.
- Brian Smith – For being my sounding wall and helping me think past my self-proclaimed limits.

- Farnoosh Brook – Showing me that passion is the driving force behind success.
- Katie West – Making me dig deeper into my beliefs than anyone has done before.
- Gretchen Rubin – Being the happiness leader that I needed in my life.
- Ryan and Larissa Smith – For being so caring.
- Jason Teitelman and Mike Williams – For being friends that always were willing to listen and support.
- Traci Fenton – For being that friend who convinced me to write this book.
- Tess Marshall – Showing me how to be more bold.
- Charlie Gilkey – Bringing me under your wing and showing me how to create systems that guide my productivity.
- Pam Slim – For you huge heart and ability to find beauty in everyone.
- To all my other friends – Your kind words have meant so much to me.

Thank you.

Now it's your turn, make a quick list of every person who has helped you succeed. Use their example to help others become happier and more successful.

Karl Staib

Visit
WorkHappyNow.com/book

**Don't forget to get the free
10 week eCourse to help you create a happier and more
successful you.**